What Makes a Great Coach?

top 10 practices of the world's best coaches

Emma Doyle
with Natalie Ashdown

Foreword by Judy Murray, OBE

For information about this title or to order other books and/or
electronic media, contact the publisher:

Open Door Press
ODP@opendoorcoaching.com.au

Library of Congress Control Number: 2022914264

ISBNs:
979-8-9852457-1-4 Print
979-8-9852457-3-8 eBook

Cover and interior design:
Scott Shaffer

CONTENTS

ABOUT THE AUTHOR

Emma Doyle

Emma Doyle is your ENERGY COACH! She is an international high performance tennis coach turned corporate coach, specialising in helping leaders and teams harness their energy, discover their purpose, and achieve high performance under pressure. She does this by inviting her clients to adopt a curious champion mindset and utilising proven coaching tools to unleash human potential.

Emma is a coach, mentor and keynote speaker who is sought after around the world. She can help you turn your motivation into actions. She is a former Division 1 U.S. college tennis player and has represented her native country of Australia as a world team coach on 20 occasions. Emma utilises the lessons that she has learned from being a high performance tennis coach and transfers these skills into her corporate coaching. She is a qualified Professional Certified Coach (PCC) with the International Coach Federation (ICF) and a Neuro-Linguistic Programming and Emotional Intelligence certified practitioner.

Emma is deeply qualified to know 'What Makes a Great Coach?' because she asks this question of all her guests on *The Coaching Podcast*. She is the host of the show and has interviewed hundreds of expert sports and business coaches, with over 30 thousand downloads to date. Emma is a TEDx speaker (*Unleashing Female Potential*) and her clients say she is the real-life female version of Coach *Ted Lasso*, believing that it is more important to be curious than judgmental. When Emma is not inspiring, improving, and impacting her clients, she can be found playing golf, tennis, pickleball and jogging/ hiking the stunning mountains where she resides in Denver, Colorado.

ABOUT THE AUTHOR

Natalie Ashdown

Natalie Ashdown is one of Australia's most senior and experienced coaches and a recognised speaker and author. Her passion, vision, creativity, and commitment assists, and supports individuals, teams, and companies to create lasting cultural change using coaching skills. Natalie is one of a small group of coaches in the world to hold the International Coach Federation Master Certified Coach credential (MCC).

Natalie often works with human resource managers, learning and development professionals, and executive teams to implement strategic initiatives and design leadership programs that target organisational change and uses coaching skills to enable change.

Natalie has designed and currently delivers, coaching qualifications that are accredited by the International Coaching Federation and form the basis of the implementation of coaching across a broad range of organisations including Australia's Defence Force. She is also sought after for her expert facilitation skills, particularly in coaching managers to coach their teams, and is regarded as a mentor by many. Natalie has worked extensively across all government levels and the private sector, with exposure and experience in international coaching including international work as a keynote speaker.

She is a qualified surf life saver, runs a surf education program for 180 children in the summer holidays, and has achieved her black belt in taekwondo.

TESTIMONIALS

'From our first moments as student and teacher, I knew Emma Doyle to be special. Her commitment, energy, and persistence to become an elite athlete, a quality coach, and a motivational speaker have been second to none. Em is a highly motivated individual, who has this uncanny ability to excite and inspire those she engages with, both as a sports coach and a public presenter. This is a book for those coaches seeking to optimise their own individual talent, both on and off the court. Certainly, to assist athletes and players to help themselves, but also a rich source of guidance for parents and business coaches in maximising high performance.'

Dr. David Parkin
Medal of the Order of Australia (OAM)
Victorian Football League (VFL) Premiership Captain – 1971
Australian Football League (AFL) Premiership Coach – 1978, 1981, 1982, 1995; and Adjunct Professor, Deakin University, Australia

'Day in and day out great coaches show up with energy, passion and a commitment to knowing their students and learning all they can to bring out their best. Emma Doyle has demonstrated these qualities since her earliest days of coaching and now she brings them to life in this book. I recommend this book to all coaches who want to grow and develop their students and most importantly, themselves.'

Nick Bollettieri
Legendary tennis coach
Founder of Nick Bollettieri Tennis Academy
(now, IMG Academy)

'We can all be better coaches and being a better coach means being a constant and consistent learner. This book puts a spotlight on what to focus on, to bring curiosity, passion, and the true love of coaching to our profession. It is inspiring, honest and heartfelt.'

Jack Groppel, PhD
Professor, Judson University and
Co-founder Human Performance Institute

'I've known Emma Doyle for many years and I have heard her speak on many occasions. Her enthusiasm and zest for life and sharing her knowledge are unmatched. Her book took me back to what's important about being a coach, including the fact that being a coach is one of the greatest gifts that lives within all of us. This book is a must-read for every coach in any sport or business and for every parent with a kid who plays a sport.'

Gigi Fernandez
Two-time Olympic Gold Medallist
Member of the International Tennis Hall of Fame

'I have the highest respect for Emma Doyle. It is rare to witness someone so devoted, enthusiastic, and driven by her passion. Despite having huge knowledge in coaching, she has always had a curiosity and humility to keep learning. That is how she can share today her years of experience.'

Patrick Mouratoglou
World-renowned tennis coach
Founder of the Mouratoglou Academy

'*Emma has devoted herself to the heart of coaching and brings decades of on-the-court wisdom to this book. Her brilliance shines brightly in the lessons and examples that she shares in What Makes a Great Coach? These lessons are very much needed as we enter into the dawn of the new age of leadership and ways of working. It is an essential read for all leaders, aspiring leaders, teams, and coaches, whether you are on the court or in the boardroom.*'

Claude Silver
Chief Heart Officer at VaynerMedia and Emotional Optimist

'*When you meet Emma Doyle, she empathises, inspires, and energises you. This book will give you tools for how she makes a difference in people. That is what I define as pure and personal coaching.*'

Emilio Sánchez
Spanish former doubles World No. 1 tennis player
Founder of the Emilio Sánchez Academy

'*There is no one else I know in the industry with as much enthusiasm and passion as Emma Doyle. A highly respected coach. I'm so excited that her book is finally here!*'

Allistair McCaw
Author, Speaker and Performance Coach
Culture and Mindset Consultant

'Emma Doyle knows what makes a great coach. Her vast amount of international experience as a coach and keynote speaker ensures she serves a lot of aces with her first book. My former doubles partner has unlocked characteristics about coaching that I guarantee will impact the journey of all coaches across the globe.'

Sarah Stone
CEO and founder of Women's Tennis Coaching Association, (WTCA)
Director of Champion Academy

'What Makes a Great Coach? is the book that we all needed when we were starting out in our coaching careers.'

Lorenzo Beltrame
President and Founder, LB Performance Solutions

'Emma Doyle is that passionate, committed, growth-minded coach that you want in your corner every single time. Her book What Makes A Great Coach? will inspire you to achieve more success while tapping into a deeper sense of joy in business, sport, and life.'

Jeff Salzenstein
Founder, Tennis Evolution
Extreme Focus Mindset Coach

'Working with Emma, I can tell you, Emma is grit, she is tough, and she works for her success. Always improving and always finding ways to help her make other peope better. Emma's coaching transcends her sport. Passion seeks an outlet, and this book is driven by that passion. If you get a chance to see Emma present, then do it. If you get an opportunity to attend her coaching clinics, then go. Read this book, then re-read it. And if you come face-to-face with Emma, the person that I have never been able to say NO to, tell her I sent you.'

Damian Camody-Stephens (Damo)
Former National Kendo Coach
Strength and Conditioning Coach

DEDICATIONS

From Emma:

I dedicate this book to my dad, Derry Doyle, for the hours that we spent playing many sports together. Your scientific approach combined with your background in psychology pushed me to challenge the status quo and that not only makes me a better coach, but also makes me a better person. Thank you for your love and support and for instilling in me a quest to conquer and nurture my inner castle.

From Natalie:

Dedicated to my dad, Leo McGuire, one of my greatest sources of inspiration, guidance, love, and support. He is the one who first introduced me to tennis and helped me fall in love with the game.

ACKNOWLEDGEMENTS

From Emma:

In 2016, I had the vision to write a book that unlocked the qualities of *What Makes a Great Coach?* That vision turned into hundreds of interviews, so I'm extremely grateful to every coach and player who shared their knowledge and wisdom to impact the quality and content within this book. Equally, I am very grateful to all my mentors along the coaching journey. You'll learn about many of them and discover their impact and wisdom throughout this book.

Also in 2016, *The Coaching Podcast* was created. On the podcast I interview expert coaches from around the world and provide practical insights for coaches and leaders to drive continuous improvement and coach for success in sport and business. My thanks to Simon Blair, one of the original co-founders, for interviewing some incredible coaches, broadening our connections, and believing in the content shared within this book. I'm so grateful to have this platform to interview expert coaches, learn from every guest, and impact the many listeners who have downloaded the podcast, over 30,000 to date.

I would like to deeply thank Natalie Ashdown, the Chief Executive Officer of The Open Door Coaching Group and my co-author. When I first met Natalie in 2007, I thought I was going to leave the tennis coaching industry altogether. I was looking for something different, so I attended Natalie's internationally recognised coaching certification. During the course she had us practice a coaching session where we were only allowed to ask questions. That was a moment in time that I will never forget.

Natalie expanded my definition of what it meant to be a coach - someone who is focused on unlocking the learning that lives within each of us. This newfound experience and many 'aha' moments catapulted me back into the tennis industry and expanded my reach as a coach and speaker in tennis, sport, and business. Without Natalie's support, guidance, and belief in my abilities, none of this would have been possible. Her ability to help bring clarity to my creative tangents and stories and her knowledge, wisdom, and experience in coaching are second to none. Thank you, Natalie, for believing in the vision of *What Makes a Great Coach?* and for always making this process such a joy.

I would like to acknowledge the unconditional love and support that I have from my family. My person, Tina Samara, who also happens to be an exceptional coach, thank you for being there every step of the way to bounce ideas off and for your unwavering support, dedication to the vision, and honesty. Thank you for sharing your knowledge as a former professional tennis player, semi-pro golfer, 11 years as a Division 1 U.S. college coach and now helping student-athletes from all over the world find college scholarships.

To my dad, Derry Doyle, who is mentioned several times in this book, thank you for always being there for me and for the wisdom that you bring to my life. Mum, Denise Doyle, you are the kindest person I know, and you are my rock. And to my entire extended family, thank you for embracing the person, the Crazy Aunty Em, and me as a coach.

From Natalie:

My acknowledgement goes to Emma for allowing me to be a part of this amazing journey. I have loved reminiscing about my early days of tennis; I've reflected on my own coaching style and practices and learned so much from our energising conversations. I have appreciated your passion, resilience, and patience throughout the countless hours we have spent on the book together. And most importantly, I've had the absolute pleasure and privilege to partner with you to bring *What Makes a Great Coach?* to life.

In addition, I'd like to acknowledge the Open Door Coaching team and our amazing clients, colleagues and friends. Thanks for bringing out the best in me.

FOREWORD BY JUDY MURRAY, OBE

I met Emma Doyle many years ago after she contacted me - from Australia - to tell me about her Girl Power camps. I'm always curious to see and hear new ideas and because I'm keen to promote and encourage female coaches, I invited her to Scotland to showcase her program and her methodology. I was impressed by her endless energy, her desire to help girls succeed in tennis...and her out-of-the-box thinking. There are not that many female coaches out there and I saw in her a kindred spirit. We formed a friendship and a working relationship that has endured and has helped to grow the girls' game worldwide.

Six years later, *What Makes a Great Coach?* is hitting the headlines and the bookshelves and I'm delighted to endorse it. Any coach can run an activity, but the great coaches know how to adapt their content, communication, and behaviour to get the best out of whoever is in front of them, and they succeed in creating learning environments that allow players to thrive.

So, this is not a book about how to hit a forehand and it is not filled with technical teaching. *What Makes a Great Coach?* focuses on what you bring to the table - the passion, the intuition, the nurturing skills, and the personality traits that can set you apart as a coach in your sport and in the business world.

Emma has researched over 500 coaches and players and this, along with her years of experience, allows her to make it clear for us what makes a great coach. Her book asks lots of important, reflective questions and really makes you think about the why and the how of enabling high performance, regardless of the industry that you are in and your role - from the front-line manager to the board room.

Truly great coaches are lifelong learners - always evaluating and analysing their sessions, listening to, and observing others, studying the latest technologies and products, and investing in their personal growth.

The book highlights the key qualities to focus on so that you build a strong foundation from the outset and be a life-long learner.

Emma doesn't just talk the talk; she walks the walk. She is one of the most dynamic EDUTAINERS I have ever met. That's someone who educates and entertains at the same time. I call her the *effervescent Aussie* because of her boundless energy and passion. If you want to know *What Makes a Great Coach?* start turning the pages. She knows what she's talking about, and I guarantee you will be EDUTAINED.

Judy Murray
Officer of the Order of the British Empire

Being the Best Coach You Can Be

'Talent is not nearly as important as execution.'

Roger Crawford
Motivational Speaker and Possibility Coach

> I want to be
> the best coach
> I can be

My first coaching experience was in Melbourne, Australia, at a local tennis club. At fourteen years old, all I wanted to do after school was play sport, especially tennis. Being child number three in a family of four siblings meant that my parents could barely afford one tennis lesson per week. Furthermore, in the mid-1980s, my moneymaking options were either working at the local fast-food outlet or delivering newspapers. I had chosen the latter and was getting paid $7.00 per round that took me three afternoons a week to complete.

Business-minded even at that age, I was painfully aware that this path did not give me a great return on investment for the time and effort I was putting into the job. My tennis coach suggested that if I began tennis coaching two nights a week, instead of the paper round, I could earn the equivalent pocket money and he would provide an extra private lesson to me at no charge. It was such an amazing opportunity that I was keen to start the very next day. When he agreed, *my coaching journey began.*

The next afternoon, I arrived at the courts feeling a sense of nervousness and excitement whilst trying not to show it.

I was ***trying to act professional.*** I had even spent time the night before applying white shoe polish to the tips of my Dunlop Volley runners to ensure they looked extra clean because I saw clean, white shoes as a sign of professionalism. ***With very little guidance and no lesson plan, I simply decided to trust my gut*** and strode out on the court to greet six children of various shapes and sizes.

'Good afternoon, I'm Coach Emma,' I announced to the group, ***liking the ring that 'Coach Emma' had to it.*** 'I'm your new coach and I can't wait to play tennis with you and have some fun. Who's up for that?' Six enthusiastic tennis racquets sprung into the air. In no time, balls were flying all over the court.

Whilst I was in fact copying the activities of the coach on the court next to me and thinking of the lessons that I had received myself, I was delighted by how the children responded to my energy and how much I enjoyed the experience. The impact of this first coaching experience was so powerful that I walked off the court with the firm conviction: ***I want to be the best coach that I can be.***

> *Have you maximised your potential?*

Armed with my new motivation to become the best coach that I could be, I started to observe other coaches. But it wasn't until several years later that I met David 'Parko' Parkin, who gave me insight into how I could get closer to my goal. **David Parkin** is a former Australian League Football (AFL) player and legendary AFL coach. At the time he was head coach of the Carlton Football Club - my favourite team since the age of five.

Halfway through my first year at Deakin University, in Melbourne Australia, studying for my sports coaching qualification, I was summoned to Parko's office because he wanted to discuss an essay that I had written on 'being the best coach'. Throughout my high school years, *I had occasionally found myself in the principal's office.* This was partly because skipping Italian class to work on my tennis skills was, in my opinion, time well spent. In this situation, finding myself standing in Parko's office, I had no idea what was coming next. He peered over his half-rimmed glasses, and in his deep, husky voice, challenged me with the following question, 'Emma, *do you really want to become the best coach that you can be?'*

'Yes, absolutely, this is *what I want to do for a living.'* I replied without hesitation.

'Well then, Emma,' he continued, 'before you can be the best coach, I need to know whether you have maximised your playing potential? *Have you gone as far as you can go in tennis?'*

The question surprised me. I wanted to blurt out 'of course', but I paused for a moment to reflect on my tennis career to date.

I had not had much success in my early junior days at the national or state levels, because I was smaller in build, not as powerful, and simply not as talented as other girls my age. However, in my mid to late teen years, I caught up in height and strength to some of the other girls in my age group. When they were beginning to develop other interests and dropping out of tennis, my skills were increasing dramatically.

I also grew up at a local club called Maribyrnong Park Tennis Club in Melbourne, Australia, that had a healthy, fun, team-based, and social atmosphere. Some of my closest friends today are the people that I grew up with from this club. This meant that during my final years of high school studies, I played some of my best tennis and was physically the fittest I had ever been. Having said that, *whilst my tennis was improving at an accelerating rate, the odds of playing at a Women's Tennis Association (WTA) professional level were unfortunately, unlikely.*

As I sat quietly in his office, reflecting, I replayed Parko's question over and over: *Have you maximised your potential?*

> *Unfinished business to see how far I can go*

I knew *I had unfinished business with tennis* and my love of the game was still alive, unlike so many of my previous rivals and teammates. Therefore, I surprised even myself with the response to the question. 'Parko,' I said, 'I haven't maximised my playing potential. I have unfinished business.' Parko nodded slowly, waiting for me to continue. *'I am good enough to play U.S. college tennis,' I said, 'and I want to see how far I can go.'*

In truth, I had no idea if I was good enough to play college tennis, but within four weeks, I was on a plane to Nashville, Tennessee. I had applied for and secured a full scholarship to play tennis for Middle Tennessee State University (MTSU). This was my first solo adventure and from the very first day it was a memorable one.

It took me 56 hours to travel from Melbourne to my destination, as the connecting flight from Chicago to Nashville was unable to take off because of thick and heavy snow. Not realising that the airline would have paid for my overnight accommodation in a hotel, I attempted to sleep at the gate of my departing flight with my arms tightly wrapped around my tennis racquet bag.

As I'm sure you can imagine, the next morning my eyes were bloodshot and my hair dishevelled. When coach Short picked me up that morning, I can imagine him thinking, 'My goodness, who have we recruited?'

But he didn't let on and instead gave me a warm Southern smile combined with a slow and steady drawl that made me feel at ease.

Playing college tennis was one of the most rewarding and memorable experiences of my late teen years. I have continued to encourage the U.S. college tennis pathway for many junior players to help them maximise their playing potential. It is a *great way to see how far you can go in the sport, whilst playing for a team and continuing your education.*

Unlocking the answers within the person	Upon reflection, Parko was doing what I would refer to as unlocking the learning that lies within the person. He asked a powerful question and then waited for me to reflect and answer the question. *He allowed me to find the answers within myself, rather than expressing his opinion first and telling me what to do.*

This type of coaching is different from the traditional sports coaching approach, where the coach sits on the sidelines or in the balcony observing the player, and then gives directions to the player based on the coach's technical knowledge.

The reason this book came to fruition	Parko's approach in the classroom was not the 'in your face' yell-and-tell approach that he might have been known for on the sporting field and is often associated with sports coaching. Instead, it was an approach based on *trust that the person in front of you has the answers.* Whilst Parko's approach may not have been in the best

interests of the university - encouraging a student to leave his coaching course - he had my interests at heart.

Tennis sporting legend and champion of equality, **Billie Jean King** said what makes a great coach is 'a great teacher'. I am grateful to Parko for his teachings and this key coaching moment that generated my call to action to head to the U.S.; and I am extremely grateful that he continues to be a mentor in my life.

Parko's question did more than set me on a journey of maximising my potential as a college tennis player; *it lit a flame of curiosity within me.* I wanted to know more about the craft and tools of coaching and in particular *'what makes a great coach?'* This became my lifelong pursuit and the reason that this book has come to fruition.

Over the past seven years I have asked more than 500 of the world's top tennis, sport, and business coaches and even some World No. 1 players: 'What makes a great coach?' Whilst the majority of the coaches came from tennis (328 coaches), my research included responses from 71 sports coaches across 21 different sports; and 105 business coaches. 48 different countries were represented in the responses which included equal representation of genders (51% female, 49% male), and one non-binary person.

From the conversations, 151 different characteristics were stated in the answers to 'What makes a great coach?' However, after collating the data, I narrowed these down to the ten top characteristics, or as I call them, ***practices, that we can all pursue.***

Whether you're a sports coach, a corporate coach, a senior leader, a manager, or a parent, you play a role in coaching the people around you; we all do.

The purpose of this book is to take you on a journey of reflection so that you can maximise your potential as a coach and answer the question for yourself: 'What makes a great coach?'

Why is this so important?

Why is this so important? Well, all the greatest coaches I have interviewed are fascinated about developing a better understanding of people, including themselves.

They're also on a pursuit of lifelong learning as mentioned on *The Coaching Podcast* by Master Professional Coach, **Jorge Capestany**. And they each want to be remembered as *a person who enabled their players to grow and develop, not only as players but as inspirational people.*

The same goes for our workplaces today. Regardless of what work we do or what industry we're in, as a leader or manager, we need to grow and develop our people, to enable them to achieve high performance. It isn't enough anymore to just direct and tell people what to do.

We need to drive innovation, accountability, and performance in workplaces. A focus on the practices I describe in the book will enable you to do that, regardless of your workplace.

> **What the corporate workplace can learn from tennis**

With that in mind, I encourage you to reflect, rather than just read the table of contents and say, 'I do that' or 'I know that.' *The corporate world can learn a lot from the world of tennis.*

What I have done through my research is synthesise the top ten characteristics or practices that make a great coach. These are the ten practices that rated highest when I consulted over 500 sports coaches, business coaches, and players. *If over 500 world-class coaches have these practices in common, then we can learn from them, regardless of our managerial level or the company we work for or the industry.*

> **How the book is structured**

As I mentioned, the corporate world can learn a lot from elite tennis and high-performance tennis coaching, so in each chapter, I have shared a *personal story and my learnings and experience* about becoming a better coach over the past 30 years. My co-author Natalie Ashdown's experience in *corporate coaching and her substantial knowledge about training managers to coach at an international level for the past 20 years, is also reflected throughout the book.*

In addition, whilst we have structured the book to give you examples from tennis that illustrate the principles of what makes a great coach, it's most important and valuable that you know how these practices can be applied to your workplace. So, in each chapter we explore *what the practice is, why it is important to the workplace, and how we can build the practice to be better coaches.*

I have also included insights and quotes from many of the people I interviewed throughout my travels. Many of these people are featured on *The Coaching Podcast* - my podcast which has gone from strength to strength and has clocked up over 30,000 listens. These guests include current and former elite coaches to the World No. 1s and other professionals at the pinnacles of their careers.

At the end of each chapter, you'll find key questions to enable you to reflect on the practices. As tennis coach and parent of professional player Kim Birrell, **John Birrell** suggests, a great coach is a *non-stop learner.* This idea is further supported by the following coaches who responded that a great coach is on a continuous learning journey. They include corporate coach **Steve Barlow;** organisational transformation coach **Charles Hardman;** tennis coach **Chie Tougas** and tennis/yoga coach **Margit Bannon.**

Therefore, the more time that you take reflecting and answering the questions, the more value you'll get from this book; and you will also be building your coaching knowledge.

So...not a tennis coaching book

So just to be clear, this is not a tennis-coaching book. Whilst I am drawing on my research from over 500 of the world's leading coaches, and I will use the word 'players' in the tennis context, it's your job to apply the lessons to your own context - business, work, home - and to your own 'players' whether they are your *clients, team members, subordinates, work colleagues, or children. Enjoy your coaching and exploring what makes a great coach.*

Your reflection | Take some time to reflect on the following questions and jot down notes below in this book or in a coaching journal. Let's start with the Parko question and some others to get you thinking:

What is holding you back from maximising your potential?

What is your inner voice saying?

What are you doing to maximise your potential?

Who do you need to become to get where you want to go?

Who can help you?

What can you take action on that is within your control?

Practice 1:
Decision-making

'It's important for a player to problem-solve...even though you (the coach) know the answers, you know the information, and you want to give it to them quickly, unless they make the decisions themselves, they are not going to make the changes.'

Alicia Molik
Former WTA World No. 8 tennis player and
Australia Federation Cup captain

Decide to make your dreams come true

I feel very fortunate that my hometown of Melbourne, Australia, is the home of the Australian Open Grand Slam and National Tennis Training Centre. Yet, despite having the opportunity to observe great players and coaches in action on home soil, I also felt that there was another world of tennis just waiting to be explored. My dream was to watch, to listen, to record key lessons, and to learn and analyse players and their games through the eyes of international expert coaches on their home courts. So, I decided to set about making that dream a reality and head to Florida.

It was 1998, and while email addresses had been around for a handful of years, this mode of communication was limited. Whilst I was quick to get a Hotmail email account, the problem was that many other people did not yet have email addresses. I knew from my past success in gaining a full U.S. tennis scholarship that *picking up the phone was the best way to create opportunities.* Even though I didn't have any contacts in Florida, this didn't stop me from cold calling different academies to try to get an opportunity to study under one of their top coaches.

It may be hard to imagine, but I used an old-school dial-up phone to ring the Nick Bollettieri Tennis Academy (now the IMG Academy), the Harry Hopman Tennis Academy at Saddlebrook Resort, and a handful of other local academies in Florida. I phoned at 4 a.m. (Australian time) three times a week for four weeks straight. I would have called more frequently, but at the time, international phone calls were very expensive, and I already felt guilty about my parents' increasing phone bill.

The result?

Not one returned phone call and not one lead.

My heart desperately wanted to learn from coaches who had developed and were working with the best players in the world. My gut said, '*Just go and see what happens*,' and '*Focus on what you can do.*'

'What you can do,' I thought to myself, over and over and over, 'is get on a plane and just turn up on their doorsteps and ask for a job.' Even as I'm writing this, it seems incredible that these were my driving thoughts, especially considering I had no returned phone calls and not a lot of savings. But these thoughts kept looping in my mind as I stretched out on our over-sized family couch at home, wrapped up tight in a blanket, watching the US Open on television in the early cold hours of the Australian morning.

> *Watching from the sidelines just doesn't cut it*

I watched television intently, ***zooming in on the coaches of the world's best players*** as they rode the waves of emotions and points with their players. I imagined myself having conversations with the coaches to debrief the games and analyse pivotal moments, learning from them and unlocking their secrets of bringing out the best in their players.

It was during one of those stay up all night to the early morning sessions that I decided it was time - not just to watch from the sidelines in Australia.

It was time to get on a plane and become a part of that world. Watching from the sidelines was not going to cut it.

I felt the fear and I saw the concerned look on my parents' faces when I told them that I intended to fly to Florida, which back then was the tennis mecca of the world. I wanted to purchase plane tickets to start my coaching journey, with only a vague idea of how to get to my destination, no real contacts, and no accommodation. Yet, despite their worries, they encouraged me on my way with the following guiding words:

1. We love you.
2. Please take care.
3. Please do not call home unless you are in serious trouble or run out of money.
4. Please do not come home for at least 12 months (because we cannot provide financial assistance).
5. Make sure your passport has at least two years' validity (in case, for any reason, you get stuck overseas).

Create
opportunities, or
go home

Those of you who travel internationally will know that long-haul flights are tough. I know that many fellow Australians will recognise this type of trip: from Melbourne to Sydney; Sydney to Los Angeles; Los Angeles to Dallas; and finally, Dallas to Tampa, Florida - a total travel time of at least 30 hours. I arrived at Tampa airport late in the evening and used a courtesy phone to book myself a hotel room at USD69 per night. I hailed a taxi, knowing that at these rates, my savings would run out in just under four months. *I also knew that from tomorrow, I would have to create opportunities. It was as simple as that.*

The next day, I rented a car and decided to turn up on the doorstep of the Harry Hopman Tennis Academy at Saddlebrook Resort. I thought that would be the best place to start, especially considering that the academy was founded by the legendary Australian coach Harry Hopman, winner of a record sixteen Davis Cups for Australia as captain-coach.

With only an address, an oversized map, and a huge amount of excitement, I set off on my journey. I was finally taking another real step towards my dreams. But with no navigation system in my rental car, I was lost within the hour and found myself stopped at a gas station to ask for directions. Even with my Australian accent and polite smile, the guy behind the counter seemed disinterested in my predicament as he shrugged his shoulders and said in a drawl, 'Gonna have to charge you for directions.'

'Charge me for directions,' I thought to myself. 'Are you kidding me?'

As the same words came out of my mouth to the attendant, I could feel the heat coming into my cheeks and I could hear the urgency in my voice. Yet, he simply shrugged his shoulders again. I stared at him, trying to burn a hole into his conscious and then turned swiftly around and headed out the door.

> *Try not to get yourself killed*

Back in the car, I was still muttering to myself 'what a joke,' and my predominant thoughts rapidly turned into 'I told you so. What were you thinking? You can't possibly drive on the other side of the road, show up at a famous tennis academy, and actually think that you will be given an opportunity.' *The first seeds of doubt started planting themselves firmly in my mind.*

I left the gas station on autopilot and pulled out onto the left-hand side of the road, which is the side of the road that we drive on in Australia. I hit the accelerator. Suddenly, I was confronted by a huge semi-trailer truck heading straight for me and heard the urgent blast from a deep horn. I instinctively swerved hard to the right, driving over the raised concrete barrier, with the crunching of metal from the undercarriage of the car adding to the desperate set of sounds.

As I brought the car to a sudden stop, I glanced into the rear-view mirror to see the double semi-trailer disappearing at speed, with the horn still blowing to drive home the message of what could have been. My heart was pounding. With my hands clenching the steering wheel, I burst into tears. It was all too much.

It took me several minutes to pull myself together and I cautiously decided to take the next exit off the interstate. Pulling into a nearby side street I jumped out of the car, gulping the fresh air and breathing deeply to get my heart rate back under control. I pulled out the map again and tried to focus and work out where I was. *I had a hunch that my destination wasn't all that far away.*

After what seemed like ages, this hunch was confirmed by a friendly couple who were out walking their dog. The gentleman took his time to carefully explain the series of left and right turns to get to the academy and I started repeating it aloud to myself: next left, turn right, straight ahead, and the other instructions over and over. This helped me refocus, and my determination to get to the Harry Hopman Tennis Academy was renewed.

A little bit of confidence goes a long way

Finally, within about half an hour I arrived at the academy. I was immediately faced with my next challenge when I drove up to the overly lavish security gate. Winding down my window, I said in a confident voice to the sleepy-looking security guard, 'Good morning, I'm Coach Emma Doyle from Australia. I'm here for a meeting with Mr Howard Moore.'

Howard Moore was the director of tennis and whilst I had called him many times as part of my phone call strategy, he had not returned any of my messages. I didn't know if he had even received them.

'The first parking lot up ahead is full,' said the guard. 'You'll have to park in the second lot further down the road over to the left. Then it's not far to walk, second main building on the left.'

'Thanks for your help' I replied in an *overly friendly voice, whilst feeling absolutely amazed that he was going to let me just drive on to the grounds. That little bit of confidence did go a long way.*

I drove along the oak-lined sweeping driveway, parked the car, and breathed in the smell of freshly cut grass and the nearby rose garden in full bloom. I could already hear the soft thud of tennis balls being pounded on the clay courts. Something about the sound of tennis balls always puts me at ease. Considering how easily I passed through security, *I started to feel that I had arrived in a place that I belonged.* Following the directions of the security guard, I headed to the main office buildings to look for Howard Moore's office.

> A split-second decision will change everything

Arriving at the office, I announced myself to the receptionist and within moments a man dressed in all-white clothing strode through the door.

In a very thick and unique blend of British-American accent, **Howard Moore** said, 'Are you that Aussie girl who's been calling and leaving messages for me this past month? And now you're here?'

'Howard, yes, hello,' I said smiling. *'I'm Coach Emma Doyle from Australia. It's lovely to finally meet you.* Thank you for taking the time to see me,' I continued, the words tumbling out without a thought. 'I am here because I want to coach for you. I would be happy to coach for free, any day or time, in exchange for accommodation. If, after seven days, you feel that I am not a suitable fit for Saddlebrook, then I will move on.'

He considered me for what seemed like an eternity and then in his unique tone, he said, 'Okay, Coach Doyle from Australia, I'll give you a shot for seven days.'

Boom! *With that split-second decision from Howard, I had my first opportunity in Florida.* I grasped his hand in thanks - probably too tightly - and headed back to the car. Trying to act cool, reaching the car, the excitement took over and I punched the air and gave a loud 'woo hoo' that distracted the players on a nearby court.

In those seven days, I worked long hours under the intense Florida sun and immersed myself in the Saddlebrook training methodologies. One of the highlights of that week was being surrounded by champion players. I found myself running on a treadmill alongside Jennifer Capriati. Still to this day, I clearly remember watching Pete 'the Pistol' Sampras, practising his incredibly efficient serve on one of the back courts. There is still a serve development activity I use today from watching him in action.

After my first week at Saddlebrook, Howard Moore offered me a coaching position, which was what I'd wanted all along. However, I had a gut feeling that I needed to see and experience more academies before taking up a full-time position. *I needed to stretch my comfort zone again,* so I asked him if he would consider holding that offer while I continued my travels.

Interestingly, in writing this book I reached out to Howard and asked him what makes a great coach? He said, *someone who uses their 'Words with impact.'* There is no doubt that the words we choose and the decisions we make shape our destiny and impact those that we coach.

> **Without making decisions, you'll be left dreaming**

In hindsight, it's easy to spot the hundreds of different decisions that I needed to make during my travels, and the decision points that could take me in one direction or another. When you're in the moment, it can feel confusing, spontaneous, scary, or any other range of emotions. *But without making those decisions I would still be snuggled up on the couch, wishing, hoping, and dreaming.*

As a result of my experiences overseas and throughout my career, I believe that enabling decision-making skills in the people we are working with is critical; this is backed up by my research. It's simply too easy as leaders and managers to make the decisions for our team members.

We often see people deferring a decision to their manager, stating reasons such as 'that's above my pay grade,' when often *it is well within their roles and responsibilities.* They are in effect still snuggled up on the couch.

If we make all the decisions, how are our team members to learn themselves? What do they do when you are not around?

I've seen processes grind to a halt because the manager has not been around to make decisions.

> *Making decisions builds confidence and allows people to take responsibility*

In tennis, a player must make hundreds and hundreds of decisions. Therefore, it is important that decision-making is drilled into players from an early age with questions such as: Where's the ball coming from? Where are you going to hit the ball? What are you going to do next?

The players and coaches that I interviewed over the past five years consistently spoke of the ways tennis requires constant decision-making on a macro and micro level - the faster you make a decision, the better you will execute the shot. Short- and long-term decision-making skills are also important life skills on and off the court.

In the workplace, whilst people may not be making as many decisions, the need for decision-making is critical. *Allowing our team members to make decisions builds their confidence and helps them to take responsibility and accountability.* If they make the wrong decision, then depending on the situation, this can be unpacked as a learning experience, just as we see on the tennis court.

Allowing our team members to make decisions also enables them to adapt to different situations and circumstances.

This leads to a more *innovative workplace and indeed a more inspired and motivated workplace.*

It also builds their ability to *make important decisions when they count the most. And to be accountable to act on their decisions.*

Be accountable to act on your decisions

Off the court, one person in my life is constantly asking me to make decisions. He is my business mentor, leadership consultant and a leadership scientist, **Aiden M. A. Thornton**. He has a brilliant mind.

When I asked Aiden 'What makes a great coach?' he responded with:

'Wise decision-making.'

Aiden has always inspired and pushed me to make and create my destiny through wise decision-making and has encouraged me to act on my decisions. As coaches in the workplace, it's also important that *we assist our team members to act on their decisions*. I am very grateful to Aiden for his time, effort, and energy in making me a better person, coach, and decision-maker.

Be the catalyst for the sliding doors moments

The theme of decision-making is explored on *The Coaching Podcast*, via the *Sliding Doors Question*. I usually frame this question as follows: 'Tell us about a sliding doors moment - you know, when your life is heading one way and something happens or someone walks into your life and you end up turning dramatically left or right.' We will have many of these moments throughout our careers, but often there are *critical decisions we will make that send our lives in a different direction*.

One such inspirational coach who shared his sliding doors moment with me was **John Borden**, the president and chief executive officer of the Washington Tennis & Education Foundation. When John was straight out of law school and heading for a career down this path, he was introduced to a lifelong mentor, **Ajay Pant**, who is the senior director of racquet sports for Life Time health and fitness clubs.

What Ajay saw in John, besides his strong tennis-playing background, was more about his off-court skills. He observed John's people skills, his sincerity, how much he cared about his clients, and noted that he was *incredibly open to learning*.

Ajay remembers the sliding doors moment like it was yesterday, when he said, 'John, I've been in this business a long time. You bring a lot of skill sets that we don't see very often in this business. I think you will have an incredibly productive and bright future, not just on the court, but also in managing and growing people and in developing programs. If we both agree that a career in tennis is something that you feel good about, *I will commit to coaching you.*'

John agreed to Ajay's offer of coaching and mentoring and this decision has led him, over time, to dedicate his life to a career in tennis. John continues to make an impact today and he lives and breathes his top three responses to what makes a great coach? - that is, someone who listens, is prepared and sincere.

Both John and Ajay are humble and gracious coach-leaders and I'm grateful for the time that we have shared learning from each other.

As coaches in the workplace, we can influence and *be catalysts for these sliding doors moments in the people that we work with.* Or as speaker and Italian Federation Tennis coach **Donato Campagnoli** suggests, exercising the 'power to empower'. Not by telling people what to do, rather by asking great questions that assist the person in exploring opportunities they may have never explored otherwise.

This is further supported by Master Certified Coach, **Judy Sabah**, who believes that asking insightful and powerful questions allows the client the opportunity to follow their agenda during the coaching process.

Encourage reflection

On *The Coaching Podcast*, tennis coach **Chris Michalowski** is always curious about this: 'If there was something that changed the direction of your life, what was that one thing?'

Tennis coach **Kris Soutar** likes to ask his players: 'What was that moment in your life that made you go down that road that you did?'

TEDx coach **Jon Yeo** asks: 'What were the tipping points in your life and what did they mean to you?"

And executive coach **Kim Miles** is focused on: 'How do you access your intuition?'

Through these questions, the coaches are trying to encourage reflection around decision-making. Other great questions we can ask our team members to encourage decision-making are:

- What are the options?
- What are you thinking?
- What's your recommendation?
- If you were the boss, what would you do?
- What's the best way forward?

Many people in our workplace are inquisitive, insightful, open-minded, curious, and spontaneous. They no longer take the spoken word as a given and enjoy being involved in decision-making processes.

Interestingly, an individual's ownership over their decision making skills leads to accountability and encourages them to take action.

This is supported in response to our guiding question, what makes a great coach, by the founder of the Winning Summit and performance coach **Mark Jeffery**; emotional optimism coach **Claude Silver**; and the Bucket List Guy and motivational coach **Travis Bell**.

Therefore, it's important that we support and guide our team members by encouraging them to solve problems and find their own solutions. This will give them the best possible chance of learning how to make decisions in the day-to-day world and how to handle the pressures of life in and outside the workplace.

| *Your reflection* | **Now is the time to reflect on your own decision-making and in turn, how you encourage decision-making in others,** |

by answering the following questions:

What is the most courageous decision you have ever made?

How did you make that decision?

Reflect on your coaching practice. How do you encourage decision-making with team members?

How do you create problem-solving environments?

To what extent are your team members empowered to think for themselves and find different solutions?

What other great coaching questions can you ask to encourage decision-making by your team members?

What actions will you take as a result of this decision? And by when?

Practice 2: Belief

'You have to believe in yourself when no one else does, that makes you a winner right there.'

Venus Williams
Former WTA World No. 1 tennis player and
Seven-time Grand Slam tennis champion

Beyond your comfort zone is the next big opportunity

The next stop along my U.S. coaching journey was another stretch out of my comfort zone. But I knew in my heart that *beyond that comfort zone was my next big opportunity and challenge* - the Nick Bollettieri Tennis Academy. **Nick Bollettieri**, arguably the grandfather of tennis and regarded as one of the best tennis coaches of all time, was back then and still is, a game changer who created the first ever in-house boarding tennis academy.

By the time I arrived, the academy had produced numerous World No. 1s including Monica Seles, Jim Courier, and Andre Agassi. In addition, over the years he has helped shape the careers of Serena Williams, Maria Sharapova, Jim Courier, Boris Becker, Anna Kournikova, Tommy Haas, and many other tennis champions.

Bollettieri's is now called the IMG Academy and it's located in Bradenton, Florida, set on 450 acres of property. Driving into the expansive estate you get the sense that you're entering into another world, a world that is exclusively designed and focused on what you love the most - to be an elite sportsperson and coach.

From the giant 'BOLLETTIERI' sign to the stretch of tennis courts and players' facilities that include indoor courts, gyms, swimming and recovery facilities, physiotherapy, strength, and conditioning rooms, the facilities simply go on and on. I immediately had the sense that I had 'hit the big time' or that *I was in an environment that bred success in every detail of the place.*

It was breathtaking, more than I had ever imagined, and there I was, right in the heart of the home of professional tennis. In no time at all I was shaking the hand of the tennis director **Gabe Jaramillo.**

I had left many messages for Gabe, and I knew from growing up in a household of seven, including my grandad, that retrieving messages was always going to be a challenge. I ensured that they were very specifically drilled in answering the phone and what to say if anyone from my long list of people happened to call back.

I discovered during the introduction, that unlike nearly every person on my list, Gabe had rung me back; unfortunately, I didn't receive the message. I was immediately impressed that he remembered me and further explained the purpose of my visit.

I remember Gabe being short and tanned with a thick Colombian accent and dressed in a crisp navy club uniform and impossibly white sneakers. Gabe oozed professionalism with a smile that would make a dentist proud. At the same time, he was warm and welcoming. He invited me to join the academy lunchtime staff meeting.

Use humour as an ice-breaker

I walked into the lunchtime meeting room, filled with at least 40 energised Gabe look-alikes, with their impeccable attire, all speaking over the top of each other at the tops of their voices.

I felt instantly self-conscious, so *my first reaction to the commotion was to hide.* I moved the back corner of the room to find a seat, whilst nodding and smiling sheepishly, trying awkwardly to avoid what seemed like 40 pairs of eyes turning towards me. My heart was racing, and I could feel the heat rising in my cheeks as the endless supply of courage that had taken me this far had suddenly disappeared.

The room became quiet when Nick Bollettieri walked into the room. But before the meeting formally began, Gabe motioned towards me at the back of the room and called out, 'We have a coach here from Australia. Please stand up, introduce yourself, and tell us why you're here.'

I stood slowly, thankful that my shaking knees were hidden by the table in front of me. I was feeling the pressure of being the only female in the room and in the presence of the great Nick Bollettieri.

I nervously coughed into my hand to clear my throat, thinking, 'Why did you do that?' and announced, 'My name is Coach Emma Doyle. I've come to the U.S. from Australia to visit some of the best tennis academies in the world.'

Immediately and fortunately, given the state of my nerves, I was interrupted by a man, who in a booming drawl called out, 'Best academies? What other academies? There's only one academy ya'll need to know! And darn you, right here, Coach.'

At this moment the entire room exploded in laughter, and I felt the ease that humour brings.

Along with that came the comfort of being acknowledged as one of them - a coach. Their warmth and friendliness continued at the end of the meeting when many of them came up to introduce themselves.

> *Belief comes from knowing who you are and what you do*

Thinking back, another element was present in that room that I sensed from the very moment I stepped inside, in fact, from the very beginning that I ventured onto the academy grounds: a feeling of belief - not an arrogant kind of belief - more of a *self-assured, authentic, kind of belief, one that comes with the experience of knowing who you are and what you do.*

From the way people walked around the grounds to the drills and reviews of points to the high fives and slow nods, or a motivational banner across a doorway, belief was present on the courts and in the corridors of every building. The coaches in the room that day had belief, and it became increasingly clear that *their job was to instil that belief in their players.* There was no better demonstration of what it meant to see belief in action than watching the training sessions of Venus and Serena Williams.

I witnessed first-hand the hard work, sweat, and grind during the Williams sisters' early years of development and under the watchful eye of Richard Williams, their father. He peppered the training session with messages to the girls to not only reinforce his belief in them, but also to foster their belief in themselves, a belief that hard work would keep them off the streets. Dedication and persistence, even against the odds, was not only worth it, but would reap benefits.

Richard was known to have had a 74-page plan that mapped out the steps for success for his daughters. So when legendary coach Rick Macci famously suggested that Richard might just have the next Michael Jordan in Venus, he replied, 'Oh no, Brother-Man, I got me two.' *Richard believed that both of his daughters would triumph.* And if you listen to their early interviews, it was clear that the Williams sisters had the belief too - *even if the people who were interviewing them didn't share that belief.*

I watched the William sisters' sessions intensely, even writing down every drill and some of the phrases that the team around them used. It was during one of these sessions that I found a rare moment when **Serena Williams** was on her own. The rest of the team had finished for the day, and she was hanging around to hit some more serves.

When she finished, I wanted to seize the opportunity to ask her about her training sessions. I wanted to know *why* she was doing certain drills and wanted to know more about her mindset and beliefs. Instead, the conversation went more like this: 'Hi, my name is Coach Emma Doyle. I'm from Melbourne, Australia.'

Serena interjected immediately by saying, 'Oh I love Australia, especially Melbourne - it's one of my favourite places to visit. I love shopping down Chapel Street.'

> *Let other people be like you (not the other way around)*

As you can probably imagine, rather than talking drills and mindset, the conversation turned to shopping and a comparison of our favourite stores and coffee spots.

Whilst I didn't find out about her beliefs and mindset on that day, everyone can learn more by watching Serena's interviews. In one interview at age 11, Serena is asked by the reporter, 'What do you want to be when you grow up?'

Serena replies simply, 'A tennis player.' To which the reporter then asks, 'If you were a tennis player, who would you like to be like?' Serena answers, *'I'd like other people to be like me.'*

Another one of my favourite quotes from Serena is:

'I was never arrogant. I just have to believe that I'm the best.'

Now is the time for self-belief

I was incredibly fortunate during my time at the academy to spend some precious time with Nick Bollettieri and it only occurred to me recently to ask the question, 'Why did he spend this time with me?'

Well, I believe the answer was that he respected anyone who wanted to learn and grow as a coach.

At the time, I had to pinch myself at how I was embraced as *one of the coaches* but this, I told myself was not a time for self-doubt. It was a time for self-belief. I was a coach, and I was there to learn as much as I could, whilst giving back value in terms of my energy and time spent coaching the junior players.

Whilst observing Nick in action, I tried to look through his eyes. I would ask myself, 'What is he seeing?' In the player, in the strokes, in the techniques, in the behaviours and their beliefs?

It was through this observation that I picked up three key lessons about the concept of belief that I still carry in my coaching toolkit today.

The tougher the shot...the bigger the finish

Lesson 1: 'The tougher the shot, the bigger the 'what?'

Nick would ask this question repeatedly. When his player was overstretched, he would ask the player to complete the sentence. He would implore them to answer during a drill, at the point where they were completely fatigued. He would be very animated, and his Italian accent only served to reinforce the answer:

The tougher the shot, the bigger the <u>finish</u>.

'Yes, that's right!' he would yell from one end of the court to the other. 'The tougher the shot, the bigger the finish.' 'Yes, the finish! What?' he repeated as the player feebly responded, 'The finish.'

'That's right. The finish.' And he would repeat the question until the player had no choice but to complete the sentence with a bit of gusto. With every question and answer, Nick was instilling a ***belief in the player that they had the ability, and the physical fitness to mount a big finish.***

Just by training at the academy you felt important. But if you were lucky enough to be on court with Nick, he made you realise that every ball mattered. Every ball was to be hit with intensity, purpose, and belief. In addition, Nick helped players believe that ***they could achieve their dreams and goals with hard work and belief in themselves.***

Overcome unforced errors quickly

Lesson 2: Overcome unforced errors quickly

'Coach Emma, every champion that I have ever worked with,' explained Nick, as he would list a handful of names, 'when they miss a shot, they're mad that they missed that shot. Deep down, they knew that they could make that ball. But they're only upset for about three to five seconds.

Then they say, 'Nick, feed me another ball. I know I can make it. Can we repeat it again?'

This commentary from Nick has several great messages, including believing that you can make the shot, demanding excellence, having high expectations, and practicing purposefully until you achieve your goal.

It is also about ***letting go of the past as quickly as possible and being connected to what needs to be done better on the next ball.*** In that way, the unforced errors are overcome quickly, and they don't start eating away at your beliefs.

Develop a champion mindset

Lesson 3: Develop a champion mindset

Throughout his career, at the end of every lesson, Nick had the ability to make every player feel that *they can achieve anything in life and that they are already a champion.* He insisted that if they possessed a champion mindset, they are and would be a champion in life. Nick believes in his own ability unconditionally and the ability of his players and very rarely looks back.

It's our job to instil belief in our team members

The message is that as leaders and coaches in the workplace, one of our jobs is to instil belief in our team members that they are capable and that they can achieve their goals. In doing so, they are contributing to the team, business unit and organisation's goals.

A part of that process is letting go of unsupportive practices and mindsets that get in the way of high performance as individuals and as a team.

One such leader who understands and practices this is **Helen Thompson**, head of global learning and development for an international service-based company. Helen is an Open Door Coaching alumna. We met when we studied our workplace and business coaching qualification together. What does Helen believe makes a great coach? Someone who is compassionate, has empathy, and believes in themselves, their team members, and the company's purpose.

Now I appreciate that some of this talk might be a challenge when you're thinking about your workplace. But we have to remember that 'belief' rated highly as one of the top qualities that makes a great coach, including, to name a few: Former WTA World No. 35 tennis player and coach **Nicole Pratt**; chief strategy officer **Olga Harvey**; tennis coach **Steve Annacone**; financial coach **Karen Deierhoi**; teen education speaker and coach **Sacha Kaluri**; and leadership coach **Mark McGregor**.

These top coaches are instilling belief in the people that they work with. If we want to be great coaches for our people in the workplace, then belief is something that we need to work on.

Authentic belief enables high performance

Why is instilling this belief within the workplace so important? Well as Simon Sinek said, 'People will follow you if they believe what you believe.'

Our team members are looking to see if we authentically believe in the strategic direction of the organisation and in the business unit goals. If we don't believe, then it's unlikely that they will believe and do what's necessary to achieve the goals. In addition, we just cannot have high performance in the workplace if we don't believe in our team members and their capabilities.

Give people the opportunity to build experience

This leads to the next question: How do we continue to work on our own self-belief as a leader and coach and the beliefs of our team members to develop the champion mindset that is often spoken about in sport?

One of the tangible things we can focus on as leaders and coaches is to *give people the opportunity to build experience* in the work that they're doing or the new work that you want them to do. This builds confidence over time until there is a tipping point at which belief kicks in.

You probably know of several people you have asked to work at a 'higher duties level'. At the time they may not have been confident. However, as they built experience in the role, their confidence increased, and the belief followed. This idea depicted in the diagram below is a concept that I learned originally from my time working at Bollettieri's. I have adapted and developed it over many years.

How belief builds over time

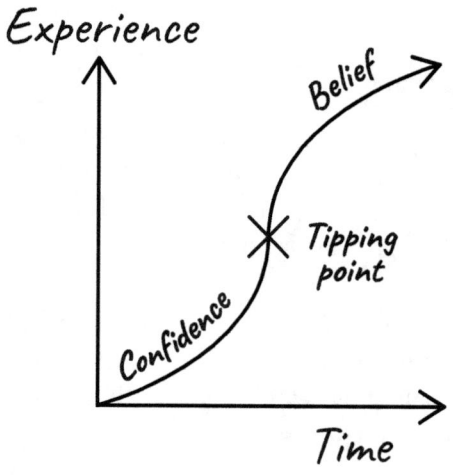

The key is that we have to believe in our team members' abilities or their ability to learn and grow first. We want to be the person that is talked about when our team members say, 'My manager thought I could do it; my manager believed in me.'

On the other hand, I know of many people who believed that they were 'ready for the next level', but for some reason or other, the manager didn't think so. By holding the person back, they are never reaching their potential.

Feelings of low motivation and 'What's the point?' kick in. People will put up with this uninspiring environment for some time, and then they will leave the organisation.

I acknowledge that it takes time to build up a person's confidence until it turns into belief, but the greatest coaches in the world instil belief in their players. In the workplace, we have to do the same with our team members if we want to ***engage people and create a high performance workplace.***

> *Build belief layer by layer – it's no different to when we were kids*

Elite cycling coach, **SyRae Weikle**, shared one of her best coaching moments. She was working with a group of 10 and 11-year-olds on their mountain bikes and the activity was riding over a long, narrow, and elevated plank.

On this particular day, the plank was 4 inches wide, 10 feet long and raised off the ground by about 6 inches. Many of the athletes were enjoying the experience, practicing the skill of balancing while riding the entire length of the plank and doing a jump off the end.

Coach SyRae then noticed one child off to the side just watching his peers. She could tell that he wanted to join in the fun, and ordinarily he loved doing jumps; however, his body language suggested that he was 'scared to have a go'.

In response she took him over to the nearby parking lot, where he followed her lead to practice riding along the white lines that made up the car spaces. It didn't take long before he had mastered this skill and felt comfortable staying on the lines while maintaining his balance.

She said to him, 'Well done! I believe in you. If you can do that, then you let me know when you're ready to give a 2-inch elevated plank a go.' She then put another plank on the car parking line that was only 2 inches off the ground. As he attempted the new elevation, she was slowly building his confidence, inch by inch.

This story is a classic example of how to **build up someone's confidence step-by-step, layer-by-layer.** It's no surprise that Coach SyRae believes someone who is genuine, confident, and caring makes a great coach.

The challenge for us as leaders and managers and coaches in the workplace is how can we build up a person's confidence, just like Coach SyRae did with her charge?

I often think that in the workplace **adults are just grown-up kids.**

What did we do to learn to ride a bike? Building confidence over time, until we found belief, is no different to other complex activities that we must learn and master in the workplace.

Let's be the coaches that enable and build belief in our team members.

Identify and leverage your superpowers (or strengths)

The other key element that I work on with my players is identifying their superpowers, refining those superpowers during their practice, and then **unleashing the superpowers during a game.**

Every great champion has weapons - think about the Federer backhand and Serena's serve. In addition, every great champion has superpowers - those intrinsic strengths that they bring to the game that makes them who they are - think about Federer's calm demeanour under extreme pressure and Serena's ability to fight her way back into a match. They are characteristics or traits or beliefs that we have about ourselves that will power us forward, in the winning moments and during the most challenging times.

Importantly, it is the coach's job to identify our players' superpowers and maximise them for high performance.

I call them **superpowers**, but in the workplace, we commonly talk about **identifying and leveraging strengths**. Research suggests that leveraging an employee's strengths in the workplace can lead to an increase in overall satisfaction, increase in innovation and creativeness, decrease in absenteeism, and a **36.5% uplift in performance.**

<table>
<tr>
<td>*Ask your colleagues and get ready to feel good*</td>
<td>If you're unclear about what your superpowers might be as a leader, manager, or coach, I recommend you simply pick up the phone and ask five of your closest colleagues or a mentor to answer the question, 'What are my superpowers?' or 'What are my strengths?'</td>
</tr>
</table>

Their responses **as a minimum will make you feel good; they might even inspire you.**

Review their responses and see if there are any similarities and then write down the qualities as affirmations. For example:

My superpower is dynamic **energy**.

My superpower is **leadership**.

My superpower is **courage**.

<table>
<tr>
<td>*Belief translates into high performance*</td>
<td>It's important to do this exercise first for yourself and then for each of your team members. As your team member taps into their superpowers or strengths, their belief in</td>
</tr>
</table>

themselves grows. A mountain of research suggests this **growth is then translated into high performance** in the workplace.

Not only that, but from my lived experience throughout my career, I've found that belief translates into high performance. And let's not forget, belief is what great coaches all around the world are instilling into their players. So, whether we use this technique or an alternative technique, we need to be doing this in the workplace.

The key is then to leverage these superpowers or strengths in the workplace for high performance.

> *It's tough when people think you're just 'big noting' yourself*

For many people, it isn't an easy exercise to identify their strengths to build belief in themselves. Particularly in some cultures, like Australia and the United Kingdom, where discussing or sharing your superpowers in a public forum can be confrontational because you look like you're 'big-noting yourself'.

Yet being able to identify your core strengths is such a necessary skill and is a fundamental element of belief.

It reminds me of a story about the time that I was facilitating a team-building day with an elite Scottish netball team. It was the first day of pre-season; there was a new coach and we had lots of fresh recruits, as this team was relatively new in the league. After starting with some rapport-building activities, we asked each player to stand up and introduce themselves along with three of their superpowers. *I made the mistake of thinking that this would be an easy exercise as they were elite athletes.* They each struggled to come up with one superpower let alone three.

However, this gave us a great opportunity to break out into small groups where each player began sharing stories about their most memorable moments on or off the court and what super power they brought to the moment that made it so special.

Through story and the power of peer-support, we began to shift the energy in the room. Also, the leaders on that day, including the inspiring CEO, **Claire Nelson**, were able to chip in and help reinforce the superpowers of the players, including some of the reasons why they had been recruited in the first place.

Claire can make you feel like you're the most important person in the room because she gives you her full attention, such an important quality when people are being vulnerable. Claire's top three responses as to what makes a great coach are vision, passion, and empowerment, empowerment being critical if you want to build belief in your people.

At this point it's worth addressing the naysayers who constantly rattle off, *'You can't just walk around saying this stuff and magically believe.'*

Well, I agree it's not about saying the statements whilst walking around like you own the world in an arrogant way. I believe in starting from a realistic mindset that allows for growth, and over time, you will adopt these strengths as your own.

I recently asked one of my players about where her belief comes from and she answered, *'It comes from the people around me telling me that I can do it and I trust them.'* This is one of the secrets to how we build belief over time.

It takes work to hold those beliefs and to avoid a negative mindset. But we can be assured that the work we do in the workplace to assist our team members around their positive beliefs will last a lifetime.

Your reflection	**Now is the time to reflect on your beliefs and how you encourage belief in others, by answering the following questions.**

Think about your beliefs and your superpowers first by answering the questions:

What are your superpowers?

How can you leverage these superpowers in your work?

Ask five people in your network to share with you what they think your superpowers are. What do they say?

What are the similarities in their responses?

Next, think about each of your team members:

What are the strengths of each team member?

How do you acknowledge the strengths in each team member?

How do you foster belief in each team member around high performance?

Practice 3: Purpose

'Everything I do has a purpose and a plan. No stone is left unturned.'

Peter McCraw
World-renowned development coach of former
WTA World No. 1 Maria Sharapova and
WTA World No. 1 Jelena Jankovic

What am I doing here?

There were times during my travels in the U.S. that I found myself wondering, 'What am I doing here?' This feeling came mostly when I was alone in my tiny one-bedroom apartment, heating two-minute noodles. Staring at the microwave as the time counted down, I found myself in a trance, only to be awoken with the 'ding' that my meal was ready.

I would peel the lid off the container and stir the noodles slowly, as if by stirring them slowly, I could evoke the feelings of a gourmet meal. Every now and then, as the steam rose, so did my tears, as I had not heard from my family in a few weeks, and I had been working long hours.

It's easy to question at this point, whether your life has become a routine of work, two-minute noodles, and sleep, on repeat. But each time I felt this way, I was able to answer the question *'Why am I here?'* and restate my purpose.

To learn from the best coaches in the world so that I can maximize my coaching potential. And I reminded myself that a lot of great coaches and players probably started out eating two-minute noodles at one point.

Think back to a time when you felt really connected

For some reason, I was reflecting on the two-minute noodle time in my career as I was waiting for a new player to arrive for our first meeting. I was excited to be meeting her and to be kicking off a goal-setting process with her, but first I wanted to understand more about *what brought her to this point and why she wanted to work with me.*

As she arrived on court, I noticed that she kicked into a routine of placing her bag down, pulling out her racquets, testing her strings, and laying out some of her gear. She rolled her shoulders and turned her head from side to side. It was only at that point, once she was ready to practice, that she came over to introduce herself. Since she was *ready to get down to business*, you can imagine her surprise, when after our introduction and a brief 'How did you go getting here?' chat, I thought I would bring up some more curious questions.

I asked her, 'Why do you play tennis?'

She looked at me strangely and I could tell she wasn't expecting the question.

'I don't know. It's fun?' she answered, but she had an inflection in her tone at the end of the sentence, as though she was looking for reassurance that this was the right answer. She started to shift her weight a little from side to side, and I got the feeling that perhaps playing tennis was not fun anymore for her, so I probed a little further.

'What do you love most about tennis?' I asked.

'Honestly, I'm really not sure,' she replied with a shrug of her shoulders.

'Can you think back to a time when you felt really connected to tennis?' I offered.

'Yes, but it was many years ago,' came the reply.

'What do you remember about those times?'

In response to this question, she perked up a little, 'I used to love competing, seeing my friends at the tournaments and playing free.' But then she looked down at her feet and let out a sigh.

'How do you feel about your tennis today?' I asked her very gently.

'Now it feels different,' she said. *'There is always so much pressure on me to perform.* I don't enjoy playing anymore. Truth be told, I still play because my parents want me to and they have put so much time and money into my tennis. *I don't want to let them down.* I don't know. I want to play. But my goals are so clouded.'

I'm sure many coaches can relate to a similar story.

We took a long time to talk about tennis and what she wanted that morning, and funnily enough we didn't even hit a ball.

> ### We have to play for the right reasons

Experienced coaches also know that only rarely will a player's goals and dreams be achieved if they are playing their sport for the wrong reasons, for example only to meet their parents' expectations. Whether it's in sport or business, *we have to play for the right reasons – the reasons that are meaningful to us.*

The good news in this story is that this player was able to take a break from the game. When she returned to tennis, focused on her own goals, she was motivated and connected to her purpose and went on to achieve a U.S. college scholarship.

> ### Why is this important to you?

Throughout my travels around the U.S., I was connecting with outstanding coaches, and it always makes me smile to think that I travelled across the world to cross paths with fellow Australian coach **Peter McCraw**.

Pete is one of the most successful coaches that I have ever come across. He has a quiet, methodical approach to everything he does; he is super detailed, and you can almost see and feel his brain ticking over; and he applies a rich foundation of science to his coaching. He is always immaculately dressed, and colour coordinated, which just rounds off his kind manner and strong coaching principles.

Pete taught me many valuable lessons and models over the years, including how to set effective goals. But before we can set our own goals or help our players set goals, we must understand our 'why' or our guiding purpose.

In conversations with Pete, he would ask, '*Can you tell me why you want to focus on this goal? Why is this important to you? What is your purpose?*'

At first, I didn't always know the purpose behind my goals or why I wanted to achieve my goals so badly. I was acting on gut instinct. But Pete kept pressing me to discover the real reason behind my dreams, goals, and motivations. In fact, I would often give him an answer relating more to the *what, how, when,* or *where* of whatever goal we were focusing on.

When I did this, Pete would dive deeper, peeling back my responses and continuing to ask questions, until we arrived at the *meaningful purpose that was driving the goal.* Questions such as: How did you feel about that? What happened? Why is this story important? What does it enable?

Pete is not alone in drilling down for a finer answer to the purpose question. Many of the coaches that I interviewed ask similar questions, not only of the people that they're working with, be it in sport or business, but also reflecting for themselves. For example:

Motivational coach **Allistair McCaw** asks: 'Why do you do what you do?'

Leadership consultant **Aiden M. A. Thornton** asks: 'What's your highest purpose?'

Professor of Sport Psychology and Coaching (track and field), **Cliff Mallett** takes it one step further by asking: 'Who is the person behind the athlete and who is the person behind the coach?'

Director of 'Thank You' products and motivational speaker **Daniel Flynn** asks: 'What's your purpose? What's the point of you being on the planet?'

Director of Sports and tennis coach **Chuck Gill** asks: 'What's your why? Why are you doing this?'

Performance coach **Lorenzo Beltrame** asks: 'What excites you when you get out of bed in the morning?'

The link to high performance

What each of these great coaches is doing is getting under the surface and finding out about the person's intrinsic motivation - their purpose and their 'why'. Or as co-founder of the Human Performance Institute, speaker and coach, **Jim Loehr** describes, finding a transcendent purpose is what makes a great coach.

Equally, we can *apply the same thinking to coaching in the workplace.* Whatever goals we're trying to achieve with our teams in the workplace, we have to start with the purpose. Call it the mission statement, vision, or any other term; it is fundamentally the 'Why are we here?' question.

Most importantly, our team members need to understand this in order to be high performing in the workplace. There is nothing more demotivating than questioning 'What's the point?' and 'Why are we doing this?' and not getting any solid answers.

You know that without a purpose and direction, the team really is rudderless. Therefore, it's up to you as a leader to engage your team in the purpose. In addition, as a coach to identify the individual's purpose and how it links to the overall team purpose to enable high performance.

A deeper intrinsic reason that can evolve over time

By the way, when you ask 'Why are you doing this?' of tennis coaches, the answer is not just *'because I will never be a World No. 1 player.'* Plenty of people would come to that realisation and then retire and do something different, other than coaching.

There is often a *deeper intrinsic reason that drives coaches, and this can evolve over time.*

This was highlighted for me during a conversation with 17-time Grand Slam winner **Gigi Fernandez**. Gigi said, 'As a former professional, I'm helping to change the perception of coaching in tennis for ex-professional players. There is the perception, as a player, that if you become a coach you have failed, because you weren't good enough or you didn't make enough money, so you had to relegate yourself to becoming a coach. But I don't feel that way.'

Gigi went on to talk about re-inventing her relationship with tennis through a sliding doors moment at an incredible event called Tennis Congress. Gigi found a large group of passionate adult recreational players who wanted to be treated like athletes. In fact, they didn't even see themselves as recreational players; they wanted the best of the best in terms of information, technology, and coaching methodologies. And they wanted to be treated the same way the professional players were treated. They were passionate about improvement and maximising high performance.

It was through discussion with these players that her new purpose beyond being a player became clear: to treat all players as professionals and with the professionalism that they deserved. And through this, her highly successful coaching business evolved.

> *Creating a legacy that inspires the next generation*

Interestingly, early in Serena Williams' journey, she is reported to have said that her goal was to simply play tennis and win tournaments. But as she became more successful, and some might say more mature, when she was asked during a press conference about goals and milestones and what was next, she would talk about a different purpose.

Her purpose evolved to ***creating a legacy that inspires the next generation of female tennis players*** and African-American athletes. She is using her success to create an impact on a global scale that is bigger than she is as an individual.

The evolution of Serena Williams' purpose can be partly attributed to her former coach Patrick Mouratoglou when he joined her team and started her thinking more about the numbers and milestones of her achievements. For example, equalling and then surpassing the number of Grand Slam tournaments won by any female tennis player in the history of the game.

At the time of writing this book Serena stands at an amazing 23 Grand Slam titles. Not only did Patrick get Serena thinking about the 'numbers', he also helped her frame *who she was becoming as an ambassador for people around the world.*

> *Take the time to unlock the purpose in each individual*

Great coaches not only know the purpose behind their bigger picture goals but the purpose of each individual activity. Most importantly, they *take the time to unlock the purpose within the individual that they're coaching.* You can do this in the workplace by asking similar questions that we've been exploring:

- What is your purpose?

- How do you walk your talk?

- How does what you're doing relate to the purpose?

- What is the purpose behind this project?

> *To execute the money shot, things need to make sense*

Sharing the purpose with team members creates an opportunity to build further connection and a sense of belonging. When activities or tasks in the workplace are connected to the purpose behind why you're doing what you're doing, you're **unlocking the potential for high performance in your team members.** Not only that, but a clear purpose supports their learning of new tasks.

People learn better when it makes sense, and it is clear to them 'why' they are doing the task and 'what's in it for them'.

For example, one of the hardest shots in tennis is hitting down the line off a ball that is coming towards you from a cross-court direction. I call this the money shot. It's thrilling to watch players execute this shot down the line. It's difficult because you have to change direction of the ball over the highest part of the net, and you have less court to hit into. It takes a lot of practice to be consistently successful and you need to execute it efficiently if you're going to make money in tennis.

To practice the shot, I ask players to rally cross-court and challenge them with the goal of attempting to push their opponent beyond the singles line, opening up the decision-making process to either hit the ball down the line or back behind the player. Why? The purpose is to encourage decision-making and to open the court and create space, which then gives you a higher chance of being successful when you take your opportunity to change the direction of the ball.

The key coaching point is **when the activity makes sense to the players** then they are more likely to engage in the activity which will transfer over onto the match court.

> *When you are on purpose, it doesn't feel like work*

In addition, it's not just our activities that need to have a purpose. When we have a sense of our own purpose and our purpose is aligned with our team, the work we are doing doesn't feel like work.

One of my mentors, **Claude Silver**, is the first ever Chief Heart Officer at VaynerMedia. Claude shares that a great coach 'has patience, empathy and takes action.'

Claude is someone whom I respect and admire because she is so clear on her purpose:

'My life's purpose is to be of joyful service and unlock emotional optimism in all.'

It takes time to state your purpose succinctly and then to unlock that in your team members. But if you do take the time you will be able to coach your team members to not only decide which goals you want to focus on each year but even more importantly, understand your 'why' behind setting them in the first place.

> *Be a part of their journey*

Of course, we can expect that our own purpose will change throughout the different chapters of our lives. As a coach we should expect this to happen with our players. There may be a time that we ***must accept that our players have outgrown us.*** In a way, I think this a real credit to our coaching - that we have achieved all we can with that player and set them up for future success. Being aware of our purpose and the purpose of our players ensures that our goals are aligned. And when we have achieved our goals together and it's time to move on, then we ***feel proud of our achievements together and celebrate along the way.***

The same applies in the workplace. I'm sure you know of people who have changed jobs and gone on to bigger opportunities. It's *nice to know that you've been a part of that journey.*

In summary, what makes a great coach is being able to help identify your team members' purpose and then to ensure that their day-to-day tasks or interactions are connected to that purpose. And as my research suggests, many of the world's best coaches agree, including: high performance tennis coach **Jim Harp**; passionate tennis player and founder of Tennis Congress **PJ Simmons**; motivational speaker and corporate coach **Carol Fox**; and tennis coach **Yasemin Ozsoy**.

So, I encourage you to have fun exploring the purpose behind your decisions, actions, and coaching. Because by focusing on yourself, learning and developing, we can unlock the high performance within our team members.

| Your reflection | Now is the time to reflect on your purpose and how you help others identify their purpose, by answering the following questions. |

Think about your purpose first by answering the questions:

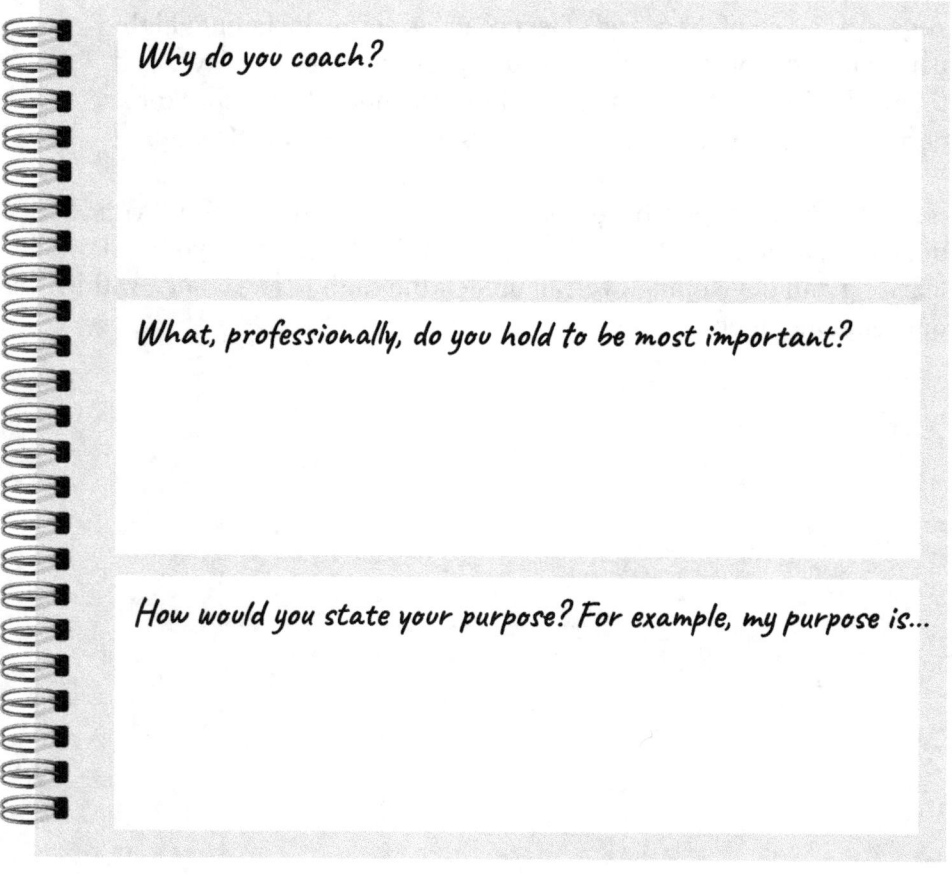

Why do you coach?

What, professionally, do you hold to be most important?

How would you state your purpose? For example, my purpose is...

Next, consider your team members:

What is important to them?

How do you help each team member identify their purpose?

How do you engage your team members to stay on purpose?

57

Practice 4: Passion

'When you are passionate, everything flows. It's a driving force. Coaching is your vocation. You know you were put on the planet to coach, and you do it because you are passionate about it.'

Emma Doyle

> *Let your imaginary crowd roar with approval*

My first real passion was Aussie Rules Football - the Australian Football League (AFL). I would kick the ball to myself, throw the ball up and mark (catch) it above my head, whilst running around the backyard. All the while, my sisters played with a tea set in the middle of the yard.

My parents recently sent me a video of me playing football in the backyard and it transported me to a magical time in the past, a time when I was imitating the great players of my favourite team, Carlton, and kicking goals into and often over, the back fence. When I kicked the ball over the fence, it was like kicking into the grandstand. *My imaginary crowd would roar with approval.*

Not so approving of my love of football was my next-door neighbour who had become accustomed to me climbing the tree in the corner of our yard to get over the fence and retrieve the ball. He would yell at me, and I would just wave and quickly leap onto the palings to scale back over the fence.

Sadly, my neighbour was not alone in his disapproval because, unlike today, girls were not allowed to play competitive team football back then. So, I moved on to playing tennis, something that I was equally as passionate about, and stuck to football just in my backyard.

> Coaching is about passion – and you'll need plenty of it to survive

With this in mind, imagine my surprise, when David Parkin strode into the lecture room in my very first university class. You will remember him from the introductory chapter. He stood at the lectern, surveyed the crowd in front of him slowly and then announced:

'Coaching is about passion. You need plenty of it if you are going to survive in this world.'

I could see his passion from the way the veins in his neck stood proud and the blood rose to his cheeks with every word as he continued to speak. The audience of eager students mumbled to each other in response; clearly it was not just me who was impacted by this first impression.

We spent the next hour with Parko, furiously scribbling down his every word. I remember my hand aching with the need to ensure I captured every morsel of inspiration.

> *The number one response when asked 'What makes a great coach?'*

When you think of legendary coaches like David Parkin, it may come as no surprise that the *number one response to 'What makes a great coach?' is passion.* Just look at some of the internationally renowned coaches who stated 'passion' as one of their answers to what makes a great coach:

Former professional tennis player, three-time NCAA team champion, two-time All-American, college coach and U.S. college recruit **Tina Samara**; tennis developer and coach **Kyle LaCroix**; former ATP No. 100 tennis player and performance coach **Jeff Salzenstein**; college coach **Bill Riddle**; tennis coach **Helen Rice**; track and field coach **Vicky Huyton**; former Australian cricket coach and corporate coach **John Buchanan**; former Director of High Performance at Tennis Canada **Debbie Kirkwood**; tennis coach and educator **Carla McKenzie**; tour coach and former coach to Justine Henin, **Juan-Pablo Abarca**; founder of the Women's Coaching Association and soccer coach **Aish Ravi**; and strength and conditioning coach **Dean Hollingworth**.

A coach is someone who is passionate. I'm sure you agree that when you say a person is passionate about something or brings passion to what they're doing, *you see it in their actions and body language; you hear it in the tone,* pitch, and volume of their voice; and you can actually feel it.

> *Continue to follow your passion, even if you're smacked in the jaw*

When I think about my early days of passion for sport, I also get drawn back to thinking about my indoor cricket final when I was twelve years old. I was fielding in the short leg position, close to the batter, when suddenly *the player hit the cricket ball right into my jaw.*

Sinking to my knees, I clutched my jaw as blood streamed from my cut lip. I stayed on my knees for what felt like ages trying to overcome the shock and gasping with pain as anxious people came from all directions to look after me.

The umpire called a timeout, and I was ushered to the bathroom by several worried parents who were trying to control the bleeding. Whilst they did a good job, if you can imagine those rugby players that return back to the field with bandages wrapped up, down, and around their heads with duct tape keeping the wads in place, that's what I looked like by the time they had finished their first aid.

Despite this, I wanted to go back out on the field as soon as the bleeding was under control because I was simply passionate about competing. *I loved the battle of competition. This battle wound was not going to stop me.* Not surprisingly, I did go back on the field, because I didn't want to let my teammates down.

Interestingly, to this day, I have no idea how the match ended but I remember the feeling of not wanting to retire. I suppose the lesson is that sometimes following your passion is going to get you hurt, but the memories, friendships, and struggles are often what binds us together. It's not the trophies that matter; it's the *passion that you bring to the relationships that really count.*

What does it mean to be passionate?

But what does it mean to be passionate? Fast forward to today, and I found myself challenged by Natalie who was asking great questions for this chapter: 'Everyone says that what makes a great coach is "passion", but what does it mean to be passionate? And most importantly, how do they bring that passion to serve their players or their team members in a corporate setting?'

The questions had been disturbing me and I took quite some time to come up with my answer (which we also used as the opening quote).

'Well…' I answered, 'When you're passionate, everything flows. *It's a driving force.* For example, when you're coaching. Coaching is your vocation. *You know you were put on the planet to coach,* and you do it because you're passionate about it.'

As I heard the words above come out of my mouth I could relax. I knew that whilst my early passion for loving the battle of competition was still well and truly alive, my passion has matured over the years.

Today, my passion is to help people love tennis and to *inspire, improve,* and *impact* coaches, players of all ages and stages, parents, and corporate people alike. And I want to *use tennis and everything I have learned about coaching at elite levels as the vehicle to unlock high potential in workplaces.*

It didn't hurt also to look up the word in the Oxford English Dictionary, which defines passion as 'any strong, controlling, or overpowering emotion or feeling, including an intense desire or enthusiasm for something; or the zealous pursuit of an aim'.

When you think across multiple sports, I'm sure you can think of many coaches and players and even players' support people and spectators whom you would describe as passionate or exuberant in a moment of time. That passion can be expressed as exuberance, enthusiasm, and love, but also as other emotions such as frustration, anger, and hate.

It's your job as a coach to work out what it is that your players are passionate about and then help them channel that passion into high performance.

> *We need passion in the workplace to ignite high performance*

The same applies to our workplaces. Workplaces would be totally boring and uninspiring if we didn't have passionate bosses and team members. *We need passion in the workplace to ignite high performance.*

Unfortunately, in today's culture, however, passion can be misunderstood as being evangelistic and zealous; often people hold back what they're passionate about for this reason. They don't speak up and when they do speak out, they are almost 'shouted down'.

As a coach, it really is our role to help a person unlock their passion and *find the best ways to communicate their passion to influence the people around them.* One of the ways that I've found useful to do this for the person I'm coaching is to either voice record or video themselves answering questions or talking about something that they're passionate about, without any filters and without holding back. Not for social media purposes, just for themselves. When they do this, you see them come alive. Then it's just a matter of how they can best communicate their passion to others.

> *Let people know that you deeply care*

As I mentioned, we've spent time thinking about what it means to be passionate because quite often it's a quality that we see in a person, and we would say, 'That person is passionate.' But what else makes up that passion, other than what we can see?

For me, it's a strong belief, something that we care deeply about, that comes from within. It's something that, when communicated with others, *they get the same feeling that you're deeply enthusiastic or care about that topic, person or thing.*

It comes as no surprise that my research also strongly indicated what makes a great coach is someone who cares.

As a coach, we must bring our passion to everything we do, whilst at the same time igniting the passion in our team members. Therefore, the natural question to ask is:

'How do you find out what a team member is passionate about?'

The process begins with asking curious questions to find out what the team member is passionate about inside and outside of the workplace.

For example, questions like:

- What did you do last weekend?
- What are your hobbies outside of work?
- How would you choose to spend time when you've got nothing on?
- Can you tell me more about what you enjoy studying?
- What books are you reading? What do you enjoy listening to?
- What are some of your favourite films or shows? And why do you like them?
- Where do you go on holidays and what do you like to do when you're there?

Once we identify what the team member is passionate about, we can then discuss how to leverage that passion to help the team member learn, develop, and enable high performance.

> Passion shows up
> in different ways

Returning to my research, I mentioned that the top answer to 'What makes a great coach?' was 'passion'. When I scroll through the list of people who said passion, including the ones listed above, I wasn't surprised to see that many of them were former and/or tour players who seek out this quality in a coach. For example, former WTA ranked No.1 tennis player **Dinara Safina**, answered 'discipline, humility, and passion' and WTA ranked No. 39 **Aleksandra Krunić** said 'knowledge, passion and understanding'.

They are all extremely passionate people themselves, but in different ways.

Passion is the reason that coaches and players stay connected to the game ; that they are prepared to train more than their opponents; they spend many months away from their families and commit to hard hours when nobody is around. We need to teach our players to harness the passion and to turn it into something that ***serves them during the game.***

It's also important to recognise how that passion translates on the court; this will vary for different players. Think of the passion that the greats of the past like John McEnroe, Jimmy Connors, and Billie Jean King brought to their game, as well as a similar passion displayed by current champions like Rafael Nadal, Maria Sakkari and Victoria Azarenka. Contrast that passion with players like Bjorn Borg, Roger Federer, Ash Barty, and Caroline Wozniacki, who showed less outward emotion, but are no less passionate.

It's the same in the workplace. Some people will go about things in a quiet way, and because they're not wearing their hearts on their sleeves, people think they don't care. It's just not true. ***People will express their passion and what they're passionate about in different ways.***

It's our job as coaches in the workplace to work that out with them and then channel that into high performance.

| *What do you care about the most?* | One way to unlock what a team member is passionate about is to ask: 'What do you care about the most?' |

I cared about the Oak Park Tennis Club in the northern suburbs of Melbourne, Australia. I had won and lost many matches over the years on those courts and there was always something easy and familiar about the courts whenever we arrived to play. So, you can imagine my dismay when I heard that this iconic club, first established in 1966, was to be **bulldozed to make way for apartment buildings**.

The club used to have 800 members, but over the years the membership had dwindled down to just 50 members. To make matters worse, the head coach role was being vacated. The previous head coach was only at the club one or two days per week, which was one of the reasons that the club had started to fall away.

The head coach is the heart of many clubs because often the first experience that a player has, when they join a club, is with the coach through taking lessons. But unfortunately, the coach didn't live locally and had responsibility for another thriving club. And since the coach wasn't at the club, there was no inflow of new members, the social environment slipped away, and the club lost the vibe that it was known for across the district.

I desperately wanted to make a difference and was inspired by the possibility of rebuilding the club, so I applied for the role of head coach. Even though I was only in my mid-twenties, I was well prepared for the interview process by sharing my vision to create a family-friendly, community hub based on the strong history of the club.

After the formal process, I was appointed as the head coach and given an immediate goal to double the membership within 12 months or the complex would be bulldozed.

I had only two clients taking tennis lessons in the beginning, but I was passionate about making the club successful once again.

> *Build a team and create an environment where people feel that they belong*

Tennis is often considered an individual sport, but every successful player has a team around them. *So, my priority was to start building a team and create an environment where people felt like they belonged.* A sense of belonging was fuelled by being passionate about the common goal to save the club.

People wanted to be around that passion, find their tribe, and rekindle their love of tennis and the club. In response, I gathered a diverse group of coaches to form a team called Tennis Innovations, with the motto 'We serve you.' As head coach, I had to lead a new culture of service that would, in a very short time, attract people to the club.

The question that we continued to ask ourselves, so that we could be of service was: 'How can we innovate so people fall in love with tennis?' In response, we were one of the first clubs to embrace the use of modified equipment to help children learn faster, more efficiently, and with greater success. The subsequent result was that they were experiencing the actual game of tennis from the very first lesson. This meant that most players had smiles on their faces and wanted to come back week after week.

Passion leads you to do extraordinary things, to go above and beyond, and to challenge the status quo.

The Tennis Innovations team channelled their passion into doing just that. We were constantly experimenting and seeking out new ways to be innovative; we held events such as a week called 'Happy Week', where the students had to dress in brightly coloured clothing, and weeks dedicated to the Formula 1 Grand Prix and Halloween. And thanks to the inspiration of Coach Norm, we even invented a Harry Potter Golden Snitch tennis activity that is still popular with kids today.

Each tennis Grand Slam was celebrated. For example, during Wimbledon you had the opportunity to learn the continental volley grip and everyone wore all-white clothing. The extraordinary thing was that we did all of this through word of mouth and old school printed flyers - there were no social media channels to spread the word.

When people came to the club, they could feel the passion. *It was something that they wanted to be a part of.* In our first year, we built the club from having just two clients to over 100 junior members and the club was saved.

Fast forward to today, I'm very grateful that one of our team coaches, Lauren Warden, is now the head coach of Oak Park Tennis Club and she continues to spread the original *Tennis Innovations* coaching methodology in being of service to the community and building lifelong tennis enthusiasts.

> 'The way we've always done it' is the sure-fire way to kill passion

As a side note, during this time I was often criticised for having themed dress-ups and playing unique games on court with the children, rather than the strict 'old school' approach to coaching tennis. But here's the thing: If the first and only experience that a lot of children have with tennis is standing in a line and having a ball tossed to them, missing, and then going to the back of the line; and doing this for 30 minutes, it is not a fun experience. No fun for the children, the coach, or the bored parents who are watching and counting how many balls their child can hit. *This activity kills passion before it even has a chance to ignite.*

If you're a sports coach, I believe that we need to take a *very careful and honest look at whether some of those 'old-style' coaching techniques create passion or kill passion.*

Same goes for the workplace. There are several activities that people are required to do that are old and tired and done because 'that's the way we've always done it'. ***Well, that is a sure-fire way to kill passion in the workplace*** - to stomp on people's new and innovative ways to get things done because it's different from the status quo.

One of the advantages that we have as coaches in the workplace is to be curious about the status quo, to ask questions, and to unlock people's ideas and options. That's the way that we ***unlock high performance, by igniting people's passions*** - and as a leader or manager, using our authority or influence to stop others from pouring cold water on other people's passions.

> A mission greater than yourself

Passion in the workplace, as it is in tennis clubs, is about ***a mission that is greater than yourself.*** It's about sharing a compelling story to encourage people to join the team. Tennis Innovations had the mission, 'Get social, be active, stay healthy, play tennis,' and it is still alive and well today.

We created a different experience, to connect children and adults with the passion of our sport. This ability to engage others in that mission is one of the reasons that we went on to successfully build four clubs with over 400 players learning how to play tennis each week.

It's no different in the workplace. What makes a great coach is someone with passion. When you're passionate, you're in service to your team and your organisation and you will unlock high performance.

Your reflection

As you've done in previous chapters, it's useful to reflect first on your own passions and then to ask the questions of your team members. Use the questions mentioned in this practice and the ones below for both purposes:

What are you passionate about?

What ignites your passion?

How did you discover your passion?

What do you care about the most?

Practice 5: Energy

'Your energy introduces you first.'

Claude Silver
Chief Heart Officer at VaynerMedia and Emotional Optimist

How many coffees have you had already?

Every time I do a presentation, people remark, 'Wow! Where do you get your energy from? What's your secret? *How do you keep your energy up?'*

For example, I remember when I was delivering a corporate clinic for Virgin Australia's Platinum Frequent Flyer customers. It was 7:05 a.m., and I was excited to be on one of the show courts at Melbourne Park, home of the Australian Open. I took a moment to recall some of the great tennis matches that I had witnessed on the court including some epic matches that involved the person I was just about to meet - superstar and former WTA World No. 1 **Maria Sharapova**.

Despite watching her train as a junior player at Nick Bollettieri's Tennis Academy and meeting her in passing on a handful of occasions, on this day I had the chance to be presenting with her.

Maria was the on-court guest. When she walked onto the court, I approached her with an outstretched hand and a beaming smile.

'Maria, good morning to you. I'm Coach Emma,' I said, introducing myself. 'I was just thinking about your incredible run of victories in 2008. You took out so many of the top players en route to claiming the title. You were in the zone. One of the best consecutive performances I've ever seen. I wish you every success in this year's event.' I was referring to Maria's 2008 Australian Grand Slam victory and the forthcoming 2009 event.

Admittedly this type of welcome might have been overwhelming, but Maria blushed and laughed and in her thick Russian accent said, 'Thank you.'

It wasn't long into the warm-up activities that she then remarked, *'I love your energy. How many coffees have you had already?'*

> *Feeling energised because I'm doing what I love*

Truth be told, I hadn't had any coffee that morning. One of my philosophies is to treat all tennis players, including the world's leading players that I'm fortunate to meet, with respect and warm Australian friendliness. Part of this philosophy is to do my research, so that I can make them feel comfortable. In addition, I didn't need coffee, because *I was also feeling energised to be out on-court with such a champion and to be doing one of the things that I really love* - sharing key leadership lessons with corporate people, using tennis as my platform.

By bringing my energy, I wanted to *create an environment that inspired the workshop participants to raise their own energy levels,* and to enable them to maximise this rare opportunity. Putting Maria at ease was one of the ways that would help facilitate the right energy for the session. After all, *no one wants a boring session at that time of the morning, with or without coffee!*

My passion for tennis and its application in the corporate world of coaching and for bringing out the potential in people that I am working with gives me my energy. It's why I jump out of bed. *I feel grateful for every day that I can do what I love.* And since doing what I love gives me so much energy and feels natural to me, it didn't surprise me that in my interviews, 'energy' was the second top response of what makes a great coach when I combined this specific description with similar coaching qualities, such as zest and enthusiasm.

Energy was featured in conversations with many people during my research, including, to name a few: motivational speaker and coach **Allistair McCaw**; World No. 1 doubles tennis player **Bethanie Mattek-Sands**; tennis legend and coach **Pat Van der Meer**, who also suggested that her husband, world-renowned tennis coach, **Denis Van der Meer,** would agree; tennis coach and sports psychologist **Julie Gordon**; entrepreneur coach **Laura Youngson**; and business executive and former NFL (football) quarterback **Oliver Luck**.

So, what specifically do we mean by energy?

| *What is energy?* |

Whilst there are mathematic definitions of energy that I don't care to remember, I've always been interested in *energy as a force* that you can often feel when you're around someone. I call it an energy signature.

For some people, this energy signature is infectious, something you want to connect and engage with. However, for others, their energy is something that you want to quickly move away from.

One coach, who epitomises someone with energy you are drawn to, is **Michele Krause**, the incredible woman who was the architect and cofounder of the Cardio Tennis program and turned it into a global trend. When I asked Michele what makes a great coach, she responded 'someone who is positive, enthusiastic and energetic.'

Michele added that, energy is tied into love and passion. ***When you love something so much and you are bringing that energy, you can transfer it to others, allowing them to take it in***, so that the energy can be reflected in one another. She went on to explain: 'You get what you give. Because if we are giving energy, we are going to get energy back and that's what makes life great.'

Everything is energy and that is all there is to it

I also relate to the words of Albert Einstein:

'Everything is energy and that is all there is to it. Match the frequency of the reality that you want, and you cannot help but get that reality. It can be no other way. This is not philosophy. This is physics.'

Growing up as the daughter of a scientist, the only times that I can recall ever being really excited about physics was when my dad and I were practising my serve. For example, to maximise my acceleration on the forward swing during my service motion, my dad and I would work on my leg drive and using the forces from the ground to create an equal and opposite reaction. In turn, this would help me to impact the ball at a higher point, creating a more energy-efficient outcome.

Fast forward to today and like many coaches, I'm constantly fascinated with the laws of motion, cause and effect, and ***how to help players become more energy-efficient.***

Regardless of the sport, great athletes have an uncanny way of knowing where they need to be in the moment and can produce graceful and efficient force. For example, watching Mia Hamm, a former American soccer gold medallist, it looks like the soccer ball is attached to her foot. Basketball legend Michael Jordan always looked to be in the right place at the right time and could hang in the air during a jump shot just before the final buzzer. Roger Federer looks like he doesn't even sweat to produce effortless force on every shot.

Martina Hingis was consistently in position before the bounce of the ball because of her ability to read the play. These champions all understand *how to maximise their physical energy.*

> *Your thoughts have energy too – be careful what you are creating*

What about the energy of the mind? What happens when we give energy to thoughts?

Neuroscientists have taught us that whether our thoughts are positive or negative, repeated thoughts strengthen the neural pathways in the brain. Interestingly, it is possible to create new neural pathways throughout your life. This can be achieved through self-awareness and a conscious effort of building new pathways. To form a new habit, it takes 21 days. For this new behaviour to become automatic it takes 66 days, according to a 2009 study published in the European Journal of Social Psychology. [1]

What's the catch when it comes to the workplace? Let's go back to Einstein's definition and read it again slowly... *'match the frequency of the reality that you want, and you cannot help but get that reality.'*

To me this means that if *we help our team members focus their energy on positive thoughts and work practices, then we cannot help but achieve that reality.*

The opposite is also true. In the workplace, if team members are focused on negative thoughts, then they are creating that reality. And we all know that positive energy builds high performance, and negativity gets in the way of high performance.

How to bring out the best energy in our team members

Given even this brief introduction to energy and its importance, the next useful questions are: How can we all do a better job of managing and maximising our energy in the workplace? And how do we coach our team members to bring their best energy, day in and day out? Let's break this question down into three categories to consider:

1. **Energy top-ups** - What tools do you have in your coaching toolkit to top-up your energy levels?

2. **Energy giving** - Who do you give your energy to and how does this energy inspire others?

3. **Energy traps** - What environments and situations drain your energy?

1. Energy top-ups

'Where do you get your energy from?' I've been asked that question so many times. But it wasn't until I began speaking professionally and watching other speakers perform, especially in the U.S., that I really sat down to think about the answer.

- What gives me energy?
- Where do I get my energy from?
- What are some of the common characteristics of great speakers?
- Where do they get their energy from?

For me, *my energy comes from loving what I do*; from interacting with people; from learning and from truly engaging with people. I get energy from listening to inspirational stories; from cooking up big ideas and from prioritising time to be still and reflect. Plus, I *get energy from seeing people succeed.*

With this in mind, one of the best things we can do with our team members in the workplace (after we have done this for ourselves, of course) is to sit down with them and *talk about what gives them energy.* It might be physical, mental, emotional, or even spiritual energy.

The key is to list those energy sources and then to work out a plan to *bring more of that energy into the workplace.* The list below provides you with some activities that might help you to top-up your energy and the energy tank of your team members:

- Buy yourself a journal and take a small amount of time in the morning (the first thing you do) or in the evening (right before you go to bed) to write three gratitude statements.

- Prioritise 30 minutes of me-time to do an activity that you loved when you were a kid.

- Adopt technology-free days or even weekends or block out certain times in your day to place your phone on 'do not disturb'.

- Plan alcohol-free days.

- Stick to some caffeine-free days.

- Address your morning and evening routines to set up your days for success.

- Do a challenging puzzle to stimulate your brain.

- Block out curiosity thinking time.

- Read or listen to something you wouldn't normally choose.

- Engage in a dialogue with friends or colleagues who think differently.

- Mix up the way you travel to work; you never know what you will discover.

- Go for a brisk walk in the fresh air.
- Take your shoes off and spend one minute connecting with the earth.
- Be aware of your nutritional habits and avoid excessive sugar intake.
- Find enjoyment in your exercise choices an accountability buddy or a community to workout with.
- Do something creative.
- Learn a new language or read about a different culture.
- Stop saying 'yes' to everything and everyone around you.
- Visualise, meditate, be still and practice being in the present moment.
- Do some recovery activities - book a massage, lie in a floatation tank or take an Epsom salt bath.

This is not an exhaustive list, but hopefully it triggered some ideas *to help you become aware of what will work best for you and your team members.* I invite you to pick three techniques and experiment with what works best. Your energy can only be restored when you have strategies that empower you to take action.

---

2. Energy giving

Another comment that is often directed my way, at the end of a training day is *'Wow! You must be exhausted.'* But for me, I'm not often exhausted at the end of a big day. Whilst passionate coaches are constantly giving energy to others, great coaches never look completely exhausted, or as though they are running on empty. The secret to this way of being is investing your energy with purpose.

When your energy is connected to your higher purpose, it's easier to say 'yes' or 'no' to opportunities. I haven't always done a great job of this in the past, saying 'yes' to everything. Consequently, I have at times become burnt out. Over time, with more clarity in your purpose, *you can choose how much and where your energy will be best served and received by others.*

In the workplace context and in sport, this means we unfortunately must accept that we cannot do the work for our team members. We need to *find the balance between how much energy to give* to team members who won't put in the effort. It can be difficult to navigate when you're invested in wanting the absolute best for your team member. But I'm sure you know the old saying: 'You can lead a horse to water, but you cannot make it drink.' Therefore, realistically, we coaches need to be smart in how we spend our time and who we dedicate our energy towards.

| *One cappuccino* |
| *please* |

On the flip side, great coaches can shift a player's energy. One word, one question, or one shift in your body language can significantly alter situations. This reminds me of a story that **Patrick Mouratoglou**, former coach of Serena Williams, shared with me. He described a player who was not playing well; it looked like she couldn't think clearly, he felt that *her energy was being poured into negative thoughts and this was impacting her play.*

It was during a WTA tournament where the coach was allowed to come out on the court twice per set during the change of ends and the player called Patrick over for some coaching advice. He went onto the court, took a chair and placed it inside the court opposite her, looked up to the umpire and said: 'One cappuccino please.'

In that moment, she initially looked perplexed, then turned towards the umpire as well and said, 'Well in that case, I will have one too please.'

Patrick was able to ***break the player's negative thought patterns, lighten up the situation, and refocus her energy.*** Doing this ultimately changed the outcome of the match to the positive.

By the way, what does Patrick think makes a great coach? 'Hear, results and expectations.' He expanded this response by saying, 'Whether you are working with males or females, you need to understand the players. You have to hear what they think, not just what they say. There is always a difference. You have to go deep into them, to get to understand (your players) and then you have a good chance to drive them to where they want to go. ***It is their car, but you have to help them drive it the right way.***'

That last comment makes sense in terms of energy - ***coaching a person to drive their energy in the direction of their goals and dreams.***

3. Energy traps

Energy traps are those things that divert our energy without really much thought. They cause us to become trapped in a pattern that ***doesn't really serve us or help us achieve our goals.*** For example, checking our phone every time it buzzes.

I was coaching a young player on the court, and they had left their phone on vibrate just on top of their bag. Without a word of a lie, I think that phone vibrated multiple times every other minute. The constant buzz alerted the player to something supposedly more important than what they were doing in that moment, which was concentrating on the player's serve.

After about ten minutes, the phone buzzed so many times, I asked the player to turn it off and put it away. It was drawing my energy away and I could feel some frustration creeping in. When the player grabbed their phone, they entered their passcode and instantly started scrolling the screen. Within a couple of seconds, they were hooked on the screen, and it wasn't until I gave them a firm 'Hey, let's go' that they snapped out of it.

Now I use the obvious example of the phone and a young player, but *we are all susceptible to this kind of activity and many other energy traps in the workplace*. When we're coaching in the workplace, the key is to identify (again first for ourselves, and then for our team members):

- What are the traps that are stealing time, focus and therefore success, away from yourself and your team members?

- When are you most susceptible to energy traps? For example when you are bored or tired or need a break?

- What commitments will you make to avoid the traps and keep yourself accountable to achieving the task at hand?

> *Create the shift in energy so that opportunities present themselves*

As leaders and managers, we can often sense that energy is lacking in the workplace. One of the jobs that we have as coaches is to help people shift their energy, to enable high performance.

One person who can help us think about this concept is **Roger Crawford**, one of the most inspiring people I have ever met. His energy is infectious, and people want to be around him.

Having been born with a severe disability, Roger went on to play Division 1 U.S. college tennis and is a USPTA certified coach. He spends most of his time traveling the world as a motivational speaker and he is the author of many books. Roger believes that along life's journey, change is inevitable.

Roger shared this wisdom in an interview on *The Coaching Podcast*, prior to the global pandemic and his wise words ring true today: 'Some people say that we are going back to normal, but if we are really lucky, we are **going forward to normal.** We have a choice. We can make something happen or we can make something out of what happens.'

He goes on to suggest, '*We can all shift our energy so that opportunities can present themselves.* Talent is not nearly as important as execution. And execution can only happen *when you direct your energy into what you want to achieve.*'

Roger does not believe in the age-old saying of 'Good things come to those who wait.' Instead, he believes, **'Good things come to people who put their energy into action.'**

Live and breathe positive energy

Another coach who has boundless energy is **Mary Pat Faley**, the director of tennis at the Riviera Country Club in Los Angeles, California. She shared with me that she loves to learn from the best coaches in the world, observe their energy, imagine the play through their eyes and listen to the subtleties within their language.

When I asked Mary Pat what she thinks makes a great coach, she responded with: someone who has 'energy, information and who is caring.'

I have seen Mary Pat in action on the coaching court and she *lives and breathes such positive energy on the court* with her body language, tone, and the way that her clients respond to this energy. Others describe Mary Pat in five words: 'a spirit of boundless energy!'

I hope that you can look around your workplace and identify someone like Mary Pat. It is that person whom we know has authentic energy, they live and breathe positivity and it's contagious.

What a sad, sad place our workplaces would be without the Mary Pats of the world.

What is even sadder is that often these positive energy people are 'shut down' because they are too 'out there' or 'too positive' or they get accused of 'being fake'. What I personally aim to do is shut down this talk and have the 'naysayer' genuinely engage with the person, so that they can ***experience what it means to have such a positive impact on the workplace and let's face it, the world in general.***

This is further supported by master professional and USPTA hall of fame coach, **Anni Miller** who believes that a great coach is, 'Real authentic'.

> *The more energy you give, the more you get back in return*

When you're connected to your higher purpose, being authentic and focus your energy for the benefits of those around you, your coaching will never feel like hard work.

Remember that everyone has an energy signature. When you meet others for the first time, you have a choice of whether or not to engage with your own energy. ***The more energy you give, the more you get back in return.***

As coaches, when we top-up our energy levels, we know that we can be the best version of ourselves possible. If we can amass, manage, and spend our energy in the same way that gravity works, amazing opportunities will flow our way. When this happens, in the workplace we can unleash high performance in the individuals and teams around us.

Your reflection

The research is clear that what makes a great coach is someone who brings a lot of energy. Therefore, this set of questions is really about your reflection on your energy and what your energy signature reveals about who you are as a coach:

What gives you energy?

What can you do to build your energy reserves?

What do you need to change?

What do you need to give up?

What do you need to do more of?

What can you do differently?

What would other people say about your energy signature?

Practice 6: Empathy

'Empathy means being able to walk alongside someone, to see them, the whole of them and then you can ask a really powerful question.'

Natalie Ashdown

Sometimes we put ourselves under too much pressure

I looked down at the little one in front of me, as her bottom lip started to tremble. She started to breathe heavily and sniff to hold back the pending flood of tears.

'Oh dear, what's wrong?' I said, as I motioned for my assistant to take over the lesson with the other players.

She looked up at me, and with a little voice that could break a heart said, *'Oh, Coach Emma, I don't think I'm ever gonna hit a backhand down the line.'*

A tiny little part of me was amused at the thought of an eight-year-old thinking her tennis days were over before they had begun.

But taking her seriously, I crouched down to her level and said softly, 'You know what…*sometimes we put ourselves under so much pressure to be the best on the court.* You know when Mum, Dad, Grandma and your rotten brother are all watching…especially when they have made it here together this time.'

She nodded and I could tell that I was on the right track. 'But do you know what?' I continued, reaching forward to whisper in her ear, 'I hit my best backhands *when I'm having the most fun.* And I heard that Ash Barty is the same.'

I paused a little to see if the message was sinking in and reached for a towel. She wiped her dripping nose and eyes and gave me a tight hug. She didn't say anything, but that hug did all the talking.

'Shall we go and have some fun?' I whispered to her again. With that she loosened her grip, she pulled her ponytail a little tighter, and we were off to hit some more backhands down the line.

Thirty minutes later at the end of the session, the same little girl was giving me another hug and pulling me down to her level. 'This has been the best day of my life,' she whispered in my ear and then it was my turn for tears.

> *No amount of 'You can do it' is going to cut it*

For this little player, as I am sure you've experienced, no amount of 'Go on. You can do it' and 'Oh, don't be ridiculous,' was going to make her tears go away, let alone motivate her to go back onto the court. In fact, I'm sure you would agree, that response would be almost heartless. Yet, I've seen children being accused of 'faking it' or feigning headaches or stomach aches to get out of tennis, all the while, parents or coaches insisting that they play on, rather than *getting under the surface to really understand what's happening with the player.*

Where is the empathy in these situations?

Another time when I had to lead with empathy was when I coached on the Junior International Tennis Federation (ITF) tour. I was often responsible for a small team of around four to six players aged between 11 and 17 years.

When coaching these players, the level of *responsibility for their entire well-being, not just their tennis, was intense.*

On one occasion with a team of four players, our flight was delayed and when it finally landed at Warsaw airport, our luggage was nowhere to be found. And our car rental booking had also somehow been lost. We were at least a four-hour drive from our accommodation and the tournament location.

Despite the rising anxiousness of my players, in a stroke of luck, I was able to secure literally the last rental car in the lot from a company. It was the equivalent of 'rent a bomb'. Ironically, we were very fortunate that our luggage didn't show up as we would not have fit five bodies and five suitcases, not to mention tennis racquet bags, into this tiny car. Finally, we were met by one of the player's long-lost relatives who we could follow to our destination. This was a big relief, as Google maps wasn't even an option back then, *yet we were somehow on the way.*

With the qualification rounds starting the next day, throughout our drive, I was sensing that the players were becoming increasingly nervous and worried - not about performing at an international level for their country - but about what they were going to wear and how this would make them look, not having all their usual equipment if their luggage didn't arrive.

Since there was nothing I could do about this in that moment, I focused on making sure they had fun on the car ride, listening to their favourite tunes, so that by the time we arrived at the hotel at around 1 a.m., they were more relaxed, albeit exhausted.

The following morning, no-one's luggage had arrived, but rather than focusing on this, we made a list of everything that was within our control. Each player had at least one racquet (thanks to taking this in their hand luggage) but there were many 'what if' questions lingering around, like 'What if I break a string?' and 'What if I'm not allowed to compete in branded clothing or casual runners?'

Firstly, it was important to demonstrate patience, ***listen to and acknowledge all their concerns***. There were lots of 'me too' sentiments. Secondly, as we asked ourselves the question, 'what was in our control?', they soon realised that none of their worries were within our control and therefore, our decisions became clearer. For example, they had to wear the clothing they wore on the plane and all of a sudden, we were off to compete.

This was a great moment for me as a coach to practice empathy, provide a safe space for everyone to contribute, voice their concerns, and then get back to focusing on the controllable things, not to mention building character at the same time.

As a coach, we quickly learn how to adapt to the circumstances that we find ourselves in and to ***lead by example to help our players cope with new environments and emotionally demanding times***. This is only possible with empathy - truly reflecting on what our players are going through at a point in time, so far away from home and adapting accordingly is key.

These moments are the stories that the players share with their family and friends when they return home and create lifelong bonds.

> *Empathy easily beats out other characteristics that you might expect*

The same concepts apply in the workplace. Think about this: When I asked over 500 coaches and players, What makes a great coach? ***empathy sits firmly in the top five in terms of responses.***

For example, empathy was mentioned by former ATP No. 1 and legendary sports commentator **Jim Courier**; along with customer experience coach **Simon Blair**; former WTA World No.4 tennis player **Helena Suková**; tour tennis coach **Carl Maes**; tennis and business coach **Scott Draper**; skill acquisition and tennis coach **Kenneth Bastiaens**; founder of Coaching Peace Consulting **Diana Cutaia**; entrepreneur, author and speaker **Manu 'Swish' Goswami**; performance coach and development manager **Belinda Colaneri**; founder of Women's Tennis Coaching Association (WTCA) and tennis tour coach **Sarah Stone**; and Australian Rules Football coach **David Wheadon**.

Empathy *easily beats out characteristics that you might expect people to nominate*, such as challenging, charismatic, confidence, dependable, dynamic, persistent, and progressive, to name just a handful. And you can be assured that *all the belief, purpose, passion, and energy in the world that you have for your sport is undermined without empathy for your team members*.

Empathy, that ability to walk in the shoes of your team members or your colleagues, to listen with all your senses and to comprehend the experiences and feelings of your team members without judgement. That's what the people around us need and want, regardless of their age, gender, and background.

Furthermore as a coach, it is *incumbent upon us to stop, pause and listen, so that we can tap into our empathy* to connect with the people we are coaching.

I understand that this isn't always easy (or even convenient) but it is also important to acknowledge that the coaching quality of patience scored highly in my research.

Practising being patient allows the space for empathy.

> *A fundamental characteristic of transformational leadership and emotionally intelligent leaders*

Further to this, the importance of empathy in the workplace was driven home to me, when I took the opportunity to interview my co-author **Natalie Ashdown** and ask her, 'What makes a great coach?'

She answered, *'Someone who brings out the best in you.'* Then I had to narrow her down to three words and she said: Empathy, listening, curiosity (meaning asking great questions with curiosity).

Taking a deeper dive into her initial answer, Natalie emphasises the importance of being able to walk alongside the person that you're coaching. She offered, 'It's more than just being able to walk in someone else's shoes, but rather being able *to walk alongside them so that you can see what they see.'*

Natalie studied empathy in leaders as a part of her doctoral studies and she suggests from an academic perspective that empathy has been described by authors as *a fundamental characteristic of both transformational leadership and emotional intelligent leaders.*

Furthermore, research by the Centre for Creative Leadership, analysing data from over 6,000 managers in 38 countries [2] found that empathy , when displayed by the leaders of organisations towards their subordinates, is *positively related to job performance and positive organisational cultures.*

The message here is clear: As coaches, our role is to demonstrate leadership to our team members. When we display empathy as a coach and a leader, this is positively related to the performance of our team members.

<table>
<tr><td>

Something I wish
I had learned
earlier in my
career

</td><td>

When I reflect on empathy across my career, I believe that *learning about empathy is what kept me in coaching; it altered the course of my coaching; and catapulted my skills to the next level.*

</td></tr>
</table>

I learned that everyone has a different 'map of the world', meaning they see the world through their eyes. Their map of the world is influenced by their values, beliefs, environment, the influential people in their lives, and the list goes on.

As coaches in the workplace, understanding our team members' maps is the cornerstone of great coaching. This means we must feel what they feel, see what they see, and especially let go of assumptions and judgments. *Something that I wish I had learned earlier in my coaching career.* This is easier said than done and is a lifelong practice.

<table>
<tr><td>

Bridging the gaps
in expectations

</td><td>

Across my tennis career, a focus on empathy has also had the single biggest positive impact on my interactions with parents. The main reason for differences of opinion between

</td></tr>
</table>

parents and coaches is a conflict between expectations and reality.

But by taking an empathetic approach, we open the opportunity for all parties to respect the perspectives of each other and *bridge the gap in expectations*, hopefully minimising conflict situations.

It's not always easy, but as a coach I aim to take the lead and *get under the surface* of the parents' concerns by asking myself several key questions:

- What are they thinking?
- Where is their motivation coming from?
- What perspective are they coming from?
- What is their map of the world?
- What is important to them? And why is this important?

I also worked out that a lot of parents want to understand the process, pathway, and structure of your program and they want nothing but the best for their child. These parents tend to communicate in a direct way, with a list of questions, and they are so appreciative when the coach takes time, step-by-step, to work through their list.

This extra time is critical and gives you an opportunity to explain your process and pathway and to clearly answer all their questions. Here's the secret: ***Once they are completely on board with your process, they will be your most loyal advocates.***

A great coach knows when they need to hold back from talking and just focus on listening. Or in the words of leadership coach, **Becky Magnotta**, 'Seek before you speak.' Even though you think you know what to say, the key is knowing when to talk and deliver a message and when to simply listen.

I've met coaches who just rely on the 'toughen up' and 'do as I say' approach, but often their players are riddled with fear because of the lack of empathy from the coach. Do these coaches create champions? The answer may be yes, but at what cost?

For every champion that is created via this approach, there are hundreds of cases where players have quit tennis; in fact, they never want to pick up another tennis racquet again.

These are the autobiographies that never get written, but if you ask any experienced coach, I bet they could easily list the names of ten players they know of who don't want anything to do with tennis anymore. This always makes me a little sad.

The previous questions and ideas are just as important in the workplace across a range of contexts.

> *Bring empathy*
> *– whether it's*
> *natural or you*
> *need to turn it on*

In the workplace some managers bring natural empathy to their approach with their team members. As customer experience coach **Jim Rembach** says, it's putting the 'person before power'. Others need to specifically turn it on and bring empathy to situations where they might not normally do so. For example, this is particularly important when there is something going on in your day or generally in your life, but you *still need to step up and coach or manage the situation.*

I was reflecting on this recently, after an exhausting and stressful day, when I had to deliver tennis lessons in the evening. With just ten minutes to spare before heading out onto the court, I stopped the car a few blocks away and took some time just to be still and focus on my breathing.

I could feel the negative energy from the day slowly releasing and as I drove the last few blocks to the courts, I refocused my attention on bringing to the court what I knew my players wanted and needed.

One of the players in this group, **Melissa Mizer**, also happens to be my running buddy and an exceptional team coach in her own right. On one of our runs after this on-court training session, I was telling her about my entire day when she remarked 'Wow! We had no idea. Your energy was the same level as it always is. *You made us feel like we were the most important players in your life.*'

This is the type of feedback that as coaches we strive for. We want our players to know that we care. As world-renowned Italian performance coach **Lorenzo Beltrame** says, a great coach is someone 'who cares for their students.' And it was no surprise that the quality of 'care' also featured strongly in my research as to what makes a great coach.

Now there will be some managers in the workplace who don't resonate with what I'm talking about because it isn't always easy for managers in the workplace to take time out. They're often feeling overwhelmed and time poor. Therefore, when they're having a difficult day themselves, it's easier to have less empathy and to think that their team members have to 'suck it up and get on with it.'

What is not easy is to stop and genuinely bring the empathy, to step into the team members' shoes, when we don't feel like it.

When you can
only imagine the
disappointment

Another great example of a coach demonstrating empathy was shared with me by **Cliff Mallett**, one of the Australian Olympic track and field coaches, who worked with Steve Brimacombe in the 1996 Olympic Games.

Steve missed out on qualifying for the final of the 200-metre sprint by three-hundredths of a second. The final turned out to be one of the most famous races, with Michael Johnson beating the world record.

Cliff knew that he had to console and speak to Steve, but he didn't know what to say. He admitted, '***How would I ever understand what Steve is feeling?***' Whilst he had experienced difficulties throughout this career, Cliff admitted that he was struggling to know how to deal with this situation and he ***could only imagine how disappointed*** his athlete would be feeling.

Unfortunately, to make matters worse, Steve had to speak to the media first. At the time there was no consideration of the impact on an athlete's mental health when forced to speak to the media after an event, particularly after a difficult loss.

This impact has only been considered in recent times when players such as Naomi Osaka have spoken out about mental health. After speaking with various media and the Australian team managers, Steve was finally able to catch up with his coach.

The whole time Cliff was thinking, 'What do I say here? How do I deal with this? Three-hundredths of a second. The guy must be shattered.' In the end, they just walked in silence around the track together, until Steve was ready to say something.

The lesson that Cliff learned was: '*I don't have to say anything. Less is more.* Just being in proximity to socially and emotionally support somebody is all you need. They just need to know that you're in their corner.'

He went on to say that we often try to 'find words and clichés that are going to help but you have to let them talk when they're ready to talk.' What a great coaching insight around the importance of bringing empathy to a challenging situation.

Empathy is something that must come from your heart, and it must be authentic. Not all of us are good at stopping and putting ourselves in the shoes of our team members, really attempting to understand their experience, whilst at the same time, putting aside our objectives and agendas. But it is incumbent upon us to find that empathy, to grow and develop our empathetic side, because empathy is the difference when it comes to what makes a great coach.

| Your reflection | The research is clear that what makes a great coach is someone who has empathy. |

Therefore, these questions invite you to reflect on your empathy:

Describe a time that you felt a person had genuine empathy for you and your situation.

What difference did it make to the situation or conversation?

Describe a time when you demonstrated genuine empathy for a team member.

What difference did it make to your team member?

What else becomes possible when you practice empathy?

Practice 7: Listening

'Listen if you want to be heard.'

John Wooden
Former UCLA basketball coach.

Someone who listens

I had the fortunate experience to be coaching at the prestigious Piping Rock Club in a stunning and very wealthy area called Locust Valley in New York. The rolling greens of the world-class golf course are set alongside the tennis courts. As I breathed in the crisp air, I smiled as I took in two of my favourite sounds in the world: the whack of golf balls and the sounds of tennis balls when they're hit perfectly in the middle of the racquet.

Not a blade of grass was out of place and the beautiful Har-Tru green clay courts were immaculately tended by a team of people who wandered the grounds primping and preening every plant, bush and tree. I arrived dressed in my Wimbledon whites as per the club policy, which also included instructions such as *'Caps are not to be worn backwards.'* I was delivering a clinic on how to run effective junior summer camps.

It was during the time of the US Open and therefore many of the professional players were in town. In fact, the Piping Rock Club had been able to engage the services of **Roger Federer**, for a pro-am member event. During the event, he was *humble and charismatic and helped many of the clearly nervous players feel comfortable*.

Incredibly, it was at the conclusion of this event that I found myself with a rare opportunity to share a brief moment with Roger on the walk from the tennis courts back to his waiting helicopter.

I had often dreamed about what I would say if I ever got the chance to talk with someone like Roger Federer, whilst at the same time *hoping that something more than gibberish might come out of my mouth.* But in that moment, I asked my guiding question:

'Roger, in one to three words, what makes a great coach?'

He paused only for a second, gave that sideways smile that he is known for, and answered, **'Someone who listens.'**

Making me feel like I am the centre of focus

I'm not sure what answer I was expecting, but Roger's answer resonated strongly with me. I thought of all the people, mentors and coaches who had influenced my life to that point. All these people have that incredible quality of *making me feel that I am the centre of focus.* They want to hear what I have to say. They let me talk things out because that's how I process thoughts and ideas. All of them are great listeners. How many hours did I spend telling my mentors about my dreams, for them to deeply listen, nod, and then add their words of wisdom to my ramblings? Too many to mention, I'm sure.

But it wasn't until I had that moment with Roger Federer that the quality became so clear to me. *I set an intention to develop my listening skills as a lifelong pursuit.*

Building on this idea, **Judy Murray**, an exceptional coach in her own right and the mother of Andy Murray, former ATP World No. 1 in men's singles and Jamie Murray, former ATP World No. 1 in men's doubles, also gave me the same answer to what makes a great coach: 'Someone who listens.'

Remember back in chapter three, when I spoke with Serena Williams' coach, **Patrick Mouratoglou**. He answered in a similar way to Roger and Judy by saying that a great coach has to 'hear, (and) hearing starts with listening.'

So too did former ATP World No. 1 doubles player **Emilio Sánchez** and former WTA World No. 27 tennis player and coach **Meike Babel**. In fact, across the more than 500 answers to our guiding question, listening was the third top response.

> *Sometimes you just gotta get in their face*

However, interestingly, people often associate coaching with the type of old-style sports coach (and there are still plenty of them around) who sits in the balcony or bunker, shouting orders down the phone, or coming down from the coach's box to give players on the field a 'spray'.

This type of sports coach basically berates their players about what they're doing or not doing and directs and tells them quite loudly exactly what they expect the players to be doing. I've even heard coaches say that they 'need to do this because it's the only thing that the player will respond to' and 'sometimes you just gotta get in their face.' Interestingly, *this style, as with many other different styles, does get results.*

Former NBA and NBL basketballer and coach, **Chris Anstey**, shared his experience of being on the receiving end of many time out 'sprays'. He said, that he didn't mind it because he knew that his coach, Brian Goorjian, cared deeply about every single one of his players. As a result, that particular team achieved a level of work ethic and results that they had never achieved previously.

Despite this stereotypical style associated with sports coaching, in my interviews of more than 500 expert coaches, *not one of them said that 'getting in the face of your player' makes a great coach.* Not one of them said 'yelling' at the player gets them the results. Yes, there are days that we all raise our voices, get frustrated and even lose our cool, but those days are hopefully few and far between.

What does Chris Anstey think makes a great coach? The 'ability to listen,' and finding the balance between when to say what.

> *The power of the pause*

Admittedly, I wasn't always a great listener nor was I skilled at being in the moment. Former World No. 1 tennis player and coach **Mats Wilander** said what makes a great coach is *'being in the present.'*

In my earlier career, I was that coach who jumped in often to solve the player's problems. Rather than asking a question and listening for the answer, I would give a rapid number of answers to the question. *I barely paused or drew a breath to allow my player to think.* In fact, I see a lot of coaches and parents behaving in this way today. Not only that, but we also see this rapid problem-solving by time-poor managers in the workplace, particularly in team meetings.

I gained a huge insight into my lack of listening skills when I needed to complete an assignment for my Sports Coaching degree at Deakin University. We had to record a coaching session and then have one of our fellow students provide feedback. I was keen to partner with **Damian 'Damo' Carmody-Stephens**, who was one of the only mature (by age) students in our course. I wanted to partner up with Damo for this assignment because I knew that his feedback would be honest, insightful, outside of the box, positive, empowering, and exactly what I needed to improve.

At the time Damo was competing in kendo and was also the Australian Kendo coach. For those of you who, like me at the time, have never heard of the Japanese martial art called kendo, it is sword fighting with bamboo sticks. In addition, Damo was one of the best strength and conditioning coaches in Australia, with a personalised approach for every athlete under his care.

After watching one of my tennis coaching lessons, Damo asked a number of questions first to seek my reflections before he offered the following powerful feedback:

'Emma remember to pause. *There is so much power in the power of a pause.'*

It took me a minute or two to process what he was saying. Then the realisation hit me. I had delivered the lesson in a way where I talked a mile a minute and I gave the learner very little time to stop, reflect, and consider any of the information. *There was no pause to allow listening when I was doing all the directing and talking.*

I expected Damo to have said that I did not stop talking for 39 minutes of a 45-minute lesson. However, he continued to say, 'Emma for your message to be powerful and for the learner to fully engage and improve, consider the amount of instruction you give, the timing, and the subsequent feedback from the learner.'

He then took a long, deep, and deliberate breath and said, 'Remember to pause Emma. *The power of the pause provides space for the learning process.'*

I've found this lesson to be so valuable on the tennis court and in the corporate world. When starting out in the coaching world, coaches often feel like they must fill the silent moments with words. But as I took more time to pause, I became a better listener and didn't need to fill in the silent moments. I know today that in fact, *it is in the quiet moments that I do some of my best coaching.* With this in mind, I am grateful to Damo who continues to be a mentor in my life. He is an exceptional person who has left an imprint on my journey.

> ### We are way too quick to jump in and solve the problem

I'm not alone when it comes to needing to develop my listening skills. My co-author **Natalie Ashdown** also admits that she was not a particularly good listener before learning how to coach effectively. Natalie, like other high performers in the workplace, would be listening to her team, whilst at the same time processing what they were saying and working on a solution.

The problem with this approach, which is common, is that you haven't fully listened to the person, nor have you given them the opportunity to come up with the solutions. *Managers in the workplace are far too quick to jump in*, cut the person off, talk over the top of them, and offer a solution. They are effectively solving a problem that they haven't even fully listened to. This is not only annoying for the team member, but it shuts down their thinking and cuts off options and discussion. *Quite often the person just gives up talking.*

Some managers even go so far as to try to finish a person's sentence. Let me be frank: *Finishing a sentence might be kind of cute with your loved ones, but in the workplace, it can be downright annoying and counterproductive.*

> ### Show them that you care

By pausing to truly listen to your team members, you can focus on what they're saying; you show them that you understand what they're saying; and if appropriate, then you can form a question in response to unlock their creativity and potential. You also get insights into their perspective, how they communicate and their level of understanding of a situation.

This allows you to coach more effectively as you adapt your coaching to meet the needs of your team member. In addition, it shows the person that you care.

It was legendary UCLA basketball coach **John Wooden** who once suggested that *one of the greatest ways to show someone you care is to give them your full attention and really listen to them.*

I experienced this firsthand when I travelled to Orlando, Florida to meet with and learn from an inspirational coach, **Jim Loehr**, who I have referenced earlier in the book. When I arrived at the Human Performance Institute, Jim's office had two sections. A desk for where he worked on one side and two comfortable chairs facing one another on the other side of the room. When he motioned for me to sit down with him on the chairs I immediately felt at ease and that he had created a safe space for listening, sharing, and learning. In that moment, I felt like I was the most important person in the room.

Listening requires us to park our ego

Another particular coach who understands the importance of listening is **Valorie Kondos Field**, affectionately known as Miss Val, who had the opportunity to learn from Coach John Wooden. Miss Val was the UCLA gymnastics coach and she shared one of her best coaching moments on *The Coaching Podcast.* At the 2018 national championships, the UCLA team were in fourth position heading into the last event, which was the balance beam, often referred to as the make-or-break event.

For each of her athletes, Miss Val had an individualized 'cue' for them that she would always remind them of right before their performance.

She went up to her first student athlete and was ready to give her the cue when suddenly the athlete grabbed Miss Val by the hand, looked at her with wonderful sparkly eyes and a majestic smile, and said, 'Miss Val, I've got this.'

Miss Val reflected that in that moment, she was smart enough to 'shut up', and just say, 'I know' and walk away and not give her the cue. Her athlete scored a personal best on beam and each of her other athletes followed suit. One by one, they all said before they performed, 'Miss Val, I'm so excited to compete. I've got this.'

Miss Val backed away, saying nothing. She *listened with her heart* and they ended up winning the national championship by the smallest of margins.

She shared with me that, 'I absolutely know, had my ego kicked in, and had I felt that they could not perform at their best without me reminding them their "cue", I know that they would have performed a little tight. They would have been over thinking and we would not have won the championship that year.' It is no surprise to hear that what makes a great coach through the eyes of Miss Val, is a coach who 'Knows thy self.'

Listening requires us to park our ego, and Miss Val's story is a great example of this in action. She also mentioned that Coach Wooden never gave advice but rather in times of pressure, he encouraged Miss Val to listen to her heart and follow its message.

Listening is not easy, particularly when even a mobile phone switched to silent will vibrate in your pocket and take your focus away from the person you're listening to. Nonetheless, listening is one of the *top skills of the world's best coaches, one that we do need to practice.*

Quieten the mind and focus on the person

So, we know that listening is important but how can we truly develop our listening skills? ***It begins with quietening our mind and focusing on the person we're listening to.*** However, sometimes rather than listening we are:

- Thinking about a response to what the other person is saying

- Waiting for our turn to talk and struggling to hold back our own thoughts

- Forming an opinion on the subject

- Only hearing what we want to hear

- Trying to solve the problem for our team members without really taking the time to understand the root cause

- Being distracted by other things in the environment or in our personal lives

It takes practice and it's a little bit hard to explain, but I breathe slowly and narrow in on the person who's talking. ***I think about the person I'm speaking with as being on the centre stage in a spotlight, with everything in the background blurred out.***

For example, when I'm on a Zoom call, I minimise my own picture or cover it with a blank document, so that I can see only the person that I'm coaching. In the workplace, this often means obvious things like turning away from your phone or a document you're working on and ***applying your focus to the person.***

How many meetings have you been in where someone is scrolling on the phone or tapping away at a laptop? And when you question what is happening, they say, 'Carry on. I'm listening.' It's not true. They are not listening.

Even worse when you're mid-sentence and the person you're speaking to answers their phone. They're effectively saying that the person on the phone, and the conversation that they know nothing about, is more important than the conversation right in front of them. Maybe they were waiting for an urgent phone call. If this is the case, then they can say that. But in my experience that situation is rare. I have said, *it's downright annoying and most people will think it's disrespectful.*

Seek to understand and clarify first

One of the other ways that we can develop our listening skills is to *ask questions first and seek to understand or clarify.*

I recently began mentoring a coach who had just been appointed the head coach of a Division 3 Women's U.S. college tennis team. He hadn't had a great college experience as a player and experienced discrimination from the coach, which consequently ended in him playing only during his freshman year. He was passionate to do things differently, but he was concerned about how to relate to the group of female players. He wanted to communicate better and to understand their worlds, including the pressures of social media.

We began by discussing the values from generation to generation and then I encouraged him to ask a lot of questions and to listen deeply to the responses, not only from the players, but from their previous coaches, their regional coaches, and their parents.

Our list of questions included:

- What are your strengths as a person, tennis player, and team member?

- What is your game style?

- How do you learn best?

- What are you working on improving?

- What information would you like to share about your past tennis history, injuries, etc.?

- When do you like to talk about the game plan for your next opponent?

- How do you like to warm up?

- What type of communication do you respond best to? In practice and in matches?

- Complete this sentence: 'I like it when my coach says...' And 'I don't respond well to comments like...'

- What type of cool-down do you normally do?

- When do you like to have a post-match debrief?

- What is your personal goal for this event?

I'm sure you will be able to modify this to your workplace context and add questions.

When we ask clarifying questions, we're gaining more information and insights. We're also showing the person that we're listening and we care.

The other big advantage is that if we listen and use the pause, then the person we're talking to may carry on talking and thinking and *find their own solution or solve their own problem.*

This kind of coaching, that leads with listening and asking questions, is more effective than jumping in and solving the problem. The person feels heard and is motivated to go away and implement what they have talked about.

As a manager in the workplace, there is nothing better. They are owning their problem and their solution. And they might even say, 'Great chat, Boss,' when all you have done is ask a couple of questions.

A critical daily practice

I can't emphasise this enough. *We have to practice our listening skills on a daily basis.* But don't just take my word for it. Take a look at some of the world's best coaches who agree that the ability to listen is one of the top critical practices in what makes a great coach. Not only **Roger Federer** and **Judy Murray** but also the director of the Victorian Tennis Academy **Tina Keown**; former professional tennis player WTA World No. 8 and Australian Federation Cup captain **Alicia Molik**; corporate leadership coach **Andy Scantland**; corporate leadership coach **Jen Brice**; former WTA World No. 29 tennis player **Urszula Radwanska**; former ATP World No. 4 tennis player **Robin Söderling**; and the list goes on and on.

As a leader, manager and coach, you want to be known as a person who listens and someone who cares. Not as a person who never listens.

This is one practice that we can all get better at and that the top coaches in the world are continuing to practice. I would go so far as to say, if one practice is going to give you more 'bang for your buck' in terms of bringing out the potential and high performance in your teams, it is this important practice of listening.

Your reflection

The research is clear that what makes a great coach is someone who listens. Therefore, these questions invite you to reflect on your own listening practice:

How would you rate yourself on a scale of 1 to 10 on how good a listener you are?

How would others rate you?

Think of a time when you felt really listened to. What were the characteristics of that conversation?

How can you bring more of those listening characteristics into your coaching toolkit?

What does deep-level listening mean to you?

How can you improve your listening skills? And by when will you act on these ideas?

Footnote for parents

My final word on listening goes to parents, specifically regarding the car ride home from tennis. I know that parents often have the urge to want to jump in and debrief immediately after a match. During the car ride home, parents often seize the opportunity to make their child listen. My advice is to not give in to this temptation. Through my observations of parents delivering post-match chats, they will often begin with, 'How do you think you played?'

As soon as they get an answer, which usually consists of something like, 'Er...all right,' or 'Not great,' the parent is off and racing with their synopsis of the match.

We all need to *take the time to listen, rather than use the car time to download.* Don't just take this from me. During the 2019 Australian Open, Rob Barty, father of former WTA World No. 1 tennis player, Ashley Barty, said that he never used to talk tennis in the car unless Ash initiated the conversation.

The best thing to do is to work out a time together for the most productive opportunity to reflect, ask questions, learn, and most importantly to listen. Encourage these environments and slowly but surely your child will share their insights, especially when you say, 'Tell me more.' The big payoffs are the connections created with your child or player - they feel heard and they develop their skills of self-awareness to improve their game.

Practice 8: Curiosity

'Be curious, not judgemental ... If you are curious, then you would ask questions.'

Ted Lasso
Played by Jason Sudeikis
Head Coach of the AFC Richmond soccer team

A dose of positivity and energy

I'm sure there are a lot of Ted Lasso fans reading this book and I just love that scene where he is shooting darts against Ruppert, and just before he hits the winning bulls-eye he says 'be curious, not judgemental.' If people are curious, rather than judgemental, then they are asking questions. This scene, along with so many others brought a dose of positivity and energy to our screens. Ted's approachable nature made us feel like he was in our lounge room, coaching us through the difficult times of the global pandemic. Personally, I found it so empowering to see a coach represented in this way, and talking about one of my most favourite practices - being curious.

How did they do that?	All my life I have marvelled at the tennis greats and wondered 'How do they do that so effortlessly?'

When you watch a winning point and hear the gasp of the crowd, followed by the thunderous applause, I'm sure that 10,000 people in the stadium and countless others at home, are saying and thinking the same thing *'How did they do that?'*

Well as it happens, my earliest memories of trying to find the answer to this question were as a ball-girl at the Australian Open.

For six years I had the most incredible opportunity to study the best tennis players in the world, from a unique perspective as a ball-girl - courtside by the net post. From this vantage point, I could see the angles, the footwork, and the strain of every muscle. *I felt the tension, smelt the sweat as they threw their towels to me,* and mopped their dripping perspiration off the lines so they wouldn't slip. I held my breath as they served so as not to even allow my breathing to get in the way of their performance. And whilst you could not see it, because we were trained to be emotionless, I really *could feel what they were feeling, and I rode every point.*

By the way, that includes feeling the searing heat of the Australian summer, back in the days when *the courts were so hot, they would literally start to melt our Dunlop Volley classic tennis sneakers* and fainting ball-kids were common occurrences. I remember trying to be first in line to replace any of these unfortunate fainting ball-kids, just to get more time out on the court studying the greatest players of that era.

During this time, my dad had a theory that following every Australian Open, despite not picking up a racquet for at least three weeks, I always played better immediately after the event. He felt that the whole experience rubbed off on me (perhaps even subconsciously) and I lifted my game to another level. I would have to agree.

Why do I need a coach when I can teach myself?

There's a lot to be said about observing the greats and being super curious about how they do what they do, then doing my best to emulate them. But today you don't have to vie for a spot as a ball-kid to learn from the greats; *it's all laid out for you on the internet.*

Type 'how to play tennis' into any internet search engine and you'll find millions of videos featuring everything from 'Learn Tennis in 10 Minutes' and 'The Ultimate Beginner Guide', to 'Tennis Etiquette' and 'Advanced Tennis Mastery'. In fact, at the time of writing, there were over 193 million videos on various forms of 'How to Play Tennis'!

In addition to this, technology has advanced to the point where you can wire a player up to a biometric feedback system to specifically analyse their every muscle movement in the pursuit of high performance.

With the abundance of information and technology available it would be easy to say, *'Why do I need a coach when I can teach myself?'* and to enjoy the kudos that people receive from being 'self-taught'. In addition, financial strains on household disposable income put pressure on the average player to justify the services of a coach. But for me the answer of 'Why do I need a coach?' is found in the concept of curiosity.

One of the critical things that videos and machines cannot do is be deeply curious about the player and their game. A machine cannot put the player at the centre of a conversation and ask insightful questions that evolve from a deep understanding about the player who's right there in front of you. Only a great coach can do that.

We must pursue being great with curiosity because I believe that in tennis many coaches are resting on their laurels, coaching from a one-dimensional perspective that treats all players in the same way - the way that I coached in the early stages of my career. Rather than pursuing personal development themselves, some coaches are relying on what has worked in the past.

Whilst some of the foundations and fundamentals of tennis coaching will never change, if this reliance solely on past methods continues, then as a coaching industry we are in danger of staying in our comfort zones.

This holds true in the workplace as well. If you continue down the path of managing your staff with directing and telling methods to educate and empower your team, your company's culture will suffer along with your bottom-line results. As a result, we know from history, *any industry that doesn't evolve and develop with the changing times risks being made obsolete.*

> *We all need to adjust our mindsets around curiosity*

However, not only coaches need to adjust their mindsets around curiosity. *Many players want their coach to tell them exactly what to do because that is the expected role of the coach.* My first real introduction to this was in U.S. college sport. Unlike the practice in Australia, in college sport, the coach is allowed to be on the court instructing the player as many times as they feel necessary. I remember my first college match when we drove south in the extremely hot and humid conditions to play against Louisiana State University (LSU).

I think because I was a freshman and it was my first competitive experience, our team coach was sitting on my court. I was losing 1-4 in the first set, and I could hear his nervous feet continuously tapping the floor. In addition, looking down the row of courts, I could see the scoreboards; they all told a similar story of a poor start for our team.

In response to his own nervousness, on a change of ends, my coach said to me, 'Just relax, everything's gonna be okay.'

I replied, 'I know coach. I just haven't had enough time to work her out yet.'

I also suggested that he may be needed on the other courts because I suspected my teammates were faltering because they were used to being told what to do by the coach. He wandered off to the other courts, started giving my teammates instructions, and their games picked up.

I didn't realise until I was reflecting on curiosity just how much some of the players depended on the coach because *their own curiosity and problem-solving skills had not been harnessed.*

However, one of my strengths as a player was to problem solve. I loved to maximise the court geometry and address what I needed to do differently to turn the score around. In the third set, I was 2-5 down and I sensed that my opponent thought the match was over. I kept the ball low and used drop shots to take her away from the baseline and out of her comfort zone. I was able to turn the match around and win the final set 7-5. Of course, not all these tight matches went my way but as this was *my first ever college match, it will always be memorable.*

Being curious sparks joy

Certainly, when I reflect on my earlier career, I was always a very curious player and coach, but this curiosity wasn't overly encouraged. I can remember asking many 'Why? Why? Why?' questions as a youngster and being told 'Because that's the way it is' or given a similar generic answer.

In addition, as a young coach, I would often sit in meetings with highly experienced coaches and *worry about asking questions.* I was concerned about other people's opinions - that they would think I didn't belong; that I was incompetent because of my questions; or worse still, that I would be laughed at.

Not only that, I compared myself to my father who was a scientist and my sister who was of the top of her class in her final year at high school, and I felt that I couldn't compete on an intellectual level.

These early concerns led me to be afraid to be curious and ask questions because *I was worried about how I stacked up compared to others. As a result, my curiosity was well and truly stifled.*

When I think about it now, I feel a sadness for my younger self - that I didn't speak up more and ask those burning questions. I'm sure now that if I did ask more questions, that no one would have laughed at me or judged me to be incompetent. But on the other hand, without these experiences, I wouldn't have learned the value of curiosity. I learned that comparing myself to others really robs me of joy; however, *being deeply curious sparks joy in me.*

The other insight that I learned was that we're all curious about different things. For me, the standard academic subjects at school didn't spark my curiosity. However, anything related to sports did ignite my curiosity. I was driven to find out more ways to improve at the sports that I loved.

I was a super curious kid with a thirst for knowledge, but I just didn't realise it at the time. It wasn't until I played college sport and sat in my favourite class called 'Coaching Philosophy' that I realised just how strong my curiosity was for coaching, and *in that environment I thrived.*

> *Don't miss the opportunity to breed curiosity*

Across the 500 coaches from my research, one of the key traits that stands out is their curiosity and in fact, curiosity was rated as the seventh top response. Tennis is a problem-solving game. *It is through our curiosity that we can solve problems and make the incremental improvements that are needed to maximise our potential.* Not only that, but we can also instil that curiosity in our players to assist them to solve problems, in practice and in the critical moments when they're on court.

The same goes for the workplace. If a manager is always directing, telling, and instructing their team members, they miss the opportunity to breed an environment of curiosity. And it is this environment that leads to the ***breakthrough improvements that build high performance in a team.***

Ken Martel, a former USA Hockey coach, supported these ideas when I interviewed him about his worst coaching moments. He said that these moments occurred when he jumped in too early to tell his players what to do. It was during these times that the player had a better idea of what to do, but it was his ego as a coach that jumped in to ***try and solve the problem for them.*** I'm sure we can all relate to these types of experiences.

> *It is impossible to know all the answers, all the time*

In the workplace, a lot of ego is tied up in being the subject matter expert and the most knowledgeable person in the room. There's also a lot of pressure associated with ***always having to know the right answer.***

In some workplaces, it's seen as a sign of weakness to not know everything. But the world's best coaches don't have this fear. ***They know that it is impossible to know all the answers, all the time.*** So, in response they are curious, and they seek information from their team members.

This is so important because it enables high performance in the team. Rather than rely on 'the Boss' for all the answers, the team members are called on to tap into their own knowledge or be curious to solve problems themselves. That's one of the most important by-products of fostering curiosity in our team members - ***we build strong decision makers.***

> *Curiosity allows natural adjustments to be made*

So how do you evoke this curiosity in yourself and in your team members in the workplace? The answer lies in **asking great questions and continuously pursuing the use of these questions to solve problems.** You can learn a lot from tennis about asking questions.

For example, when watching a player, ask yourself, 'How are they achieving that result?' or 'What specifically is causing the ball to move in that direction?' Or better still, ask the player to tune into their senses and feelings to answer the question themselves.

There is a famous video of legendary coach and 'grandfather' of modern coaching, **Sir John Whitmore**, delivering a coaching session in the workplace, using golf as a metaphor. It just so happens that a person in the group plays golf, so Whitmore encourages the person to 'coach' another member of the group who can't play golf on how to hit the ball. The team member starts giving their coachee several instructions about how to stand, how to hold the golf club, how to lean over and keep their head straight.

Meanwhile Whitmore simply says, 'Hit a couple of balls' and asks, 'How does that feel?'

In the video, *the person giving the instructions is so focused on the instructions that the person they're coaching has not even hit a ball.* In the meantime, Whitmore's student is feeling more and more comfortable as Whitmore asks questions that enable them to tune into their body, modify what they're doing naturally, and *start to make the necessary adjustments to successfully hit the ball.* [3]

Now I'm not for a second saying that in the workplace you shouldn't give instructions. Of course, you need to set direction and give the parameters or 'left and right of arc' as the coaches in the Air Force would say.

However, when you ask questions from a curious place, you can raise awareness in your team members that was not there before and unlock their learning and potential. *They can make natural adjustments.* And this awareness can make a huge difference to their performance in the workplace.

Continuously searching and looking for the edge

This idea of asking questions from a space of curiosity is supported by **Ric Charlesworth**, former coach of the Australian men's field hockey team, the Hockeyroos. Ric coached the team to a gold medal at two Olympic Games in 1996 and 2000.

When I interviewed him on the topic of curiosity, Ric said, *'As a coach, curiosity means that we need to be continuously searching and looking for the edge. It is our job to spark that in our players.'*

He went on to offer additional key questions to consider as coaches:

- What sparks your curiosity?
- What seems unlikely and impossible but if we did it, it would make a big difference?
- Where do you find the gap?

Ric's philosophy of adopting a curious mindset is further supported by another top-level coach, **Cliff Mallett**, who you will recall from the previous chapter on empathy. He is also a professor of Sport Psychology and Coaching at the University of Queensland.

I asked Cliff what he thinks makes a great coach. He answered:

- Someone who cares, treating people as people to help you understand the person behind the performer
- Challenging yourself and others
- And being *curious, being a lifelong learner*

He expanded on the latter by saying 'Great coaches are curious, lifelong learners who push the envelope. You have to find the answers to the big questions and develop this curiosity in the athletes you coach.'

In addition to his own beliefs, Cliff researched 14 of the world's most successful coaches in multiple contexts as part of the Serial Winning Coaches Project [4] and discovered three factors that reinforced the understanding about what makes coaches great. One of these is that:

'Great coaches learn all the time; they don't stop learning because they are curious.'

They want to know more than everyone else knows so that they can be the best coach they can be to help the athletes that they work with.

Cliff went on to say, 'What provides the edge is that the coaches we studied are curious. As consumers of research, they are quite critical too. They just don't take what's trendy; they interrogate it and think about how they might play with that idea or that information in their own context.'

> *Ask intriguing questions to spark curiosity*

Another coach whom I consider to be a leader in terms of inspiring curiosity is **Craig Cignarelli**. Craig is a master coach and speaker. When I met him in Los Angeles, I really felt that I was meeting a kindred spirit. Craig is a student of the *strategy* of tennis, and it was his strategic approach that I was keen to emulate.

Craig has the ability to dissect the game, the geometry of the court, and the complexity of the angles of the court. But rather than using his knowledge to tell players what to do, he *asks intriguing questions to spark curiosity in his players.*

Tennis is a game that requires you to manipulate the ball on your terms. To do this, as coaches we need to highlight the strengths of our player and expose the weaknesses of the opposition. It is only through curiosity that we can work out the strengths and weaknesses. Craig's approach to this is to ask questions that stretch the player's thinking, whilst at the same time considering the stage of development of the player.

I once brought a 14-year-old player to his club in Malibu to experience his unique style of coaching. He began challenging her immediately with questions like:

- We are in a cross-court rally and my forehand is better than yours. What are you going to do?

- If you want to land a ball in a certain place on the court, where do you need to be?

- We are in a baseline rally, and you need to hit an inside-out forehand to win the point. Where is the balling coming from? Where does your body need to be? How can you create this opportunity?

Craig would set up these different types of scenarios with his player and have them think about their body, the angles, the flight of the ball, and many other intricate details. Rather than giving his player the answers, he would describe the scenarios, create the plays, and *allow his players to work it out for themselves.* Of course, he would also share his knowledge, experience, and extensive research of the game, but rather than teaching tennis in the exact same way to each player, Craig *responds to the player in front of him with genuine curiosity about what makes them tick.*

Craig has had a significant influence on my coaching, and I often use his techniques today. This is the beauty of sharing information and taking your players to experience other coaching methodologies.

> *Don't be afraid to share information and ask questions*

This is a critical skill that the business world can learn from tennis. In the tennis world, great coaches are *never afraid to share information, watch each other coach, and ask each other for their opinions,* especially when you get stuck with a challenge, such as, whether to change someone's grip. This is such a healthy practice and one I highly recommend.

However, I've noticed that it's not really the same in the workplace. *People are too busy protecting their own path to share information.* In addition, there is an old saying, 'knowledge is power.' To have power in the workplace, some managers think you must have the knowledge, and protect it, rather than share it.

However, taking our cues from the top coaches I have interviewed, it is asking curious questions and being open to developing yourself that makes a difference. Furthermore, *when you leave your ego at the door, you enable curiosity to flourish.*

Team members flourish and are stretched to find the answers to interesting questions. This builds innovation and high performance in the workplace.

What sparks your curiosity?

By the way, if you're looking for inspiration around great questions, you can head to *The Coaching Podcast*, where the last question on every episode is when I ask the guest coach to ask us, the listeners, a question. The way that we frame this is by asking:

'What sparks your curiosity?'

Here are some great examples:

Former ATP World No. 42 tennis player, coach, and business coach **Scott Draper**: 'How do we get people to the point where their mindset is completely open to change and learning?'

Scott's brother who is also a former tennis player and coach **Mark Draper**: 'How do coaches go about managing the chemistry of the team? How do you manage the egos (often your super-stars) within the rest of the team?'

Former WTA World No. 4 tennis player **Johanna Konta**: 'I'm curious about the process; what's their approach on how to work through difficulties and triumphs?'

The importance of curiosity is also described by corporate coach **Barb Van Hare**; tennis coach **Marley Woods**; leadership coach **Jared Bull**; and co-founder of the Human Performance Institute, speaker and coach **Jack Groppel**; to name just a few.

I wonder just how far I can go?

Another lesson that I want to share with you around curiosity came through coaching an inspiring lady named Erin. I call Erin the 'dream-seeker' because not only did she want to learn how to play tennis as an adult, but she wanted to see *just how far she could go*. She was curious about what she could achieve and what was possible.

On first impressions, given that she had perfected the 'swing and miss', you might think that her tennis days were limited. *I had to suspend my judgment and assumptions about what might or might not be possible and trust my gut.* I believed in what could be possible if we partnered together.

Erin taught me as a coach to genuinely harness factors that don't fit perfectly into what we think we know about the world and to let go of being right. She sparked my curiosity to find out what she was capable of on and off the court.

Now, imagine if we did this in the workplace with all of our team members. I wonder just how far we could go.

| Your reflection | I still ask the question, 'How do they do that so effortlessly?' On top of that there are several questions that we can ask in |

our workplaces:

What am I curious about as a coach today?

What is my team curious about?

What do they want to learn about?

What are other organisations and sports doing that we can learn from?

What are other coaches doing that can be applied to my situation to help me solve problems?

Practice 9:
Communication

*'The real job (of a coach) is to understand how people
communicate because it is different for everyone.'*

**Patrick Mouratoglou
Tennis coach and founder of the Mouratoglou Academy**

> *Move, move. You
> gotta move ya
> feet*

I sat at the edge of the court, out of sight,
watching and listening to the coach yell at their
player, 'Move, move. You gotta move ya feet.'

Over and over again the coach insisted, like
an irate seagull fighting for scraps of bread,
until they said, 'Okay, bring it in. What's wrong with you today? Why
aren't you moving your feet?'

The player shrugged, 'I'm just not feeling it today' and that was the end
of the session.

The player shoved their racquet forcibly into their bag, collected
their other gear and walked off the court, leaving the coach shaking
their head and starring at their back. I sat there for several minutes
afterwards, reflecting on what I had just witnessed and wondering why I
found the interaction so jarring and uncomfortable.

Sadly, what I had just witnessed could be playing out on any court or in
any sport, all around the world. Coaches, parents, well-meaning adults
- whatever their relationship to the player - *yelling directions at their
players and expecting them to fall in line and change.*

For some players, the yelling gets through to them; but for most it just shuts them down. That's not your job - to frustrate, annoy, belittle, and shut our players down to the point that they give up and storm off the court. ***Our job, as coaches, is to communicate messages to be received in a meaningful way that builds, empowers, encourages, and grows our players.***

But why is it that we see such poor communication from coaches? Perhaps the answer lies in how we were taught ourselves in the early days of our careers.

> *A renewed focus on communication is needed*

I'm sure I'm not alone when I say that the coaching I received in my early days of tennis was mostly technique centred. As a result, I inherited a style that was focused on instruction and technique. Many parents would comment that when they came to watch me coach, ***they could hear my coaching instructions from a couple of courts away.*** While on the surface, this might sound as though I was running a great coaching session, the coach within me today reflects on those lessons and would describe them as completely one-way.

I made all the decisions for the players, whilst shouting directives and technical instructions. It was a case of rapid fire, 'Left, right, do this, do that, stop, run, pivot'… the list goes on. As I mentioned back in Practice 7 - Listening, we had to watch ourselves coach on video, as part of a university assignment, and this was the first time that I observed just how direct I was as a coach. It was a bit of a shock, but I'm reminded that self-awareness and listening to yourself coach is always the best place to begin if you want to make a change.

Little wonder I found the session I described at the beginning of this chapter so jarring and uncomfortable - I have made major changes in my coaching communication since those early days and witnessing the style once again brings up that awareness.

Turning back to my research, when I asked, 'What makes a great coach?' communication was in the top ten characteristics. In fact, if you combine the scores for communication with listening or with empathy, because both are a part of communication, then those two attributes both score higher than knowledge.

Communication was stated as one of their three top qualities by former WTA World No. 1 in doubles, tennis player and coach **Gigi Fernandez**; former WTA World No. 1 tennis player **Justine Henin**; former WTA World No. 26 tennis player, World No. 3 in doubles and media commentator **Casey Dellacqua**; AFL football coach **Jules Hay**; founder of Parenting ACES **Lisa Stone**; performance coach and psychologist **Michelle Cleere**; and NFL coach **Jay Gruden**, just to name a few.

Perhaps coaches spent a lot of time pursuing technical mastery and knowledge, rather than *empathy, listening and refining their communication skills.* Whatever the reasons, legendary tennis coach, **Nick Bollettieri**, and **Tony Palafox**, the former coach of John McEnroe, both say, we *must know our players.* As does coach education consultant and tennis coach **Anne Pankhurst**. To do so, I believe a renewed focus on communication is needed in the sports coaching world.

> *Your style did get you this far; but that doesn't make it right*

Critically it is not only sport that will benefit from improved communications and a revolution that moves from directing and telling, to what makes a great coach.

Across our workplaces, you don't need me to tell you that communication skills are vital. And just as in tennis, *many managers today grew up on an instructional and technical diet and then over time became the subject matter experts.* They might have gone on the odd leadership or management development course, but I'm sure you've seen many return from those courses unchanged.

The problem is that there was not enough emphasis on communication skills and real coaching skills that ensure managers are doing the practices described in this book! They need to be pausing and listening; they need to be demonstrating empathy and curiosity.

Instead, I've heard managers say, 'Well, my style got me this far. I must be doing something right.'

My response is, yes, your style did get you this far, but it doesn't necessarily make it right.

The biggest impact of poor communication can be seen in the conflict that it causes in the workplace. The effects that *detract from high performance can be traced back to poor communication in some way.* Consider these examples:

- A manager sent a text, when they should have emailed or phoned
- The team has too much communication over something confidential
- The team has not enough communication, meaning people feel left out
- The message got distorted
- The message didn't get delivered at all

The list goes on and on.

Natalie recalls facilitating a change management workshop where the first question she asked was 'What would you like to achieve from the workshop?'

She knew she was in trouble when several participants answered, 'We would like to know what the change is.' She hurriedly called a morning tea break to get a further debrief from the stakeholders.

Each of the stakeholders said, 'They should know about the change; we've been communicating it.' Well, the feedback in the room was quite clear - *the message had not been received.*

Communication skills are not hard; they just take practice

We urgently need an improvement in communication skills in our workplaces if we are to achieve high performance. It's as simple as that.

It was **Sir John Whitmore** who famously told Natalie, 'Coaching is not hard; it's changing our habits that is hard.'

The same can be said for communication skills - they are not hard to develop; they just take practice.

Making the big shift in coaching styles

A person who has played a vital role in challenging my beliefs around communication styles is **Dr Mitch Hewitt**. Mitch is an adjunct associate professor at the University of Canberra, Australia, and has a PhD in Teaching/Coaching/Pedagogy from the University of Southern Queensland, Australia. He is a leader is his field of pedagogy, which he explains in simple terms on *The Coaching Podcast* as the *art of teaching and coaching children.*

I had the pleasure of meeting Mitch some years ago when we were paired together as learning facilitators to run Tennis Australia's Junior Development coaching courses. Running these courses with Mitch never really felt like work. The days flew past as *we bounced ideas and curious conversations off each other and challenged ourselves to set up great learning environments for the coaches.* I was instantly magnetised by his extensive knowledge on both historical and current teaching methodologies.

The easiest way to explain Mitch's influence is by sharing how he helped me to develop my coaching communication style over time. Specifically, my style has evolved from being primarily *an instructional or directing and telling style* of communication, to more *coachee-centred and questioning style.* [5]

I remember when I first started talking with Mitch, I felt a little defensive as I always considered myself predominantly a coachee-centred coach, rather than instructional coach. However, without judgment, Mitch helped me focus on how I could really take the concepts of being coachee-centred to the next level.

With Mitch's permission, I have included some of his concepts, and adapted them for the purpose of our discussion.

By the way, Mitch talks about *direct* and *indirect* styles, but for our purposes *instructional* and *coachee-centred* coaching styles resonates with me and is more commonly used in workplace coaching so that is the terminology that I am using.

> *Most people think about an instructional style when they think about coaching*

Discussing an *instructional* coaching style of communication can often be used interchangeably with terms like directing and telling, explicit, teacher-centred, prescriptive, or command and control.

An instructional style is characterised by the coach making most of the decisions regarding the *how, why,* and *what* of the player's learning, whilst the player closely follows the coach's commands and directions. Communication is one-way and revolves around the coach's knowledge and instruction, with the coach explaining, demonstrating, organising, and conducting the lesson in addition to providing feedback in order to correct players' errors.

This is a highly structured and controlled instructional environment. In addition, the communication has a highly active teaching focus. *The player's success is based on the coach communicating instructions and the coachee following the instructions.*

During my eight years on the tour, I witnessed hundreds of coaches who used the instructional coaching style in their communication. *In fact, when most people think about coaching, this is the style they think about.*

While there are, of course, many success stories that come from this communication style, I expect that there are hundreds or even thousands of unhappy stories that you will never know about.

One of the main causes for this unhappiness is that when the coach uses only this communication style combined with a lot of negative commands, it serves to impact the player's inner voice. For example, I've heard a coach say:

- You look like you have concrete in your shoes! Why aren't you moving your feet? I've told you to move!

- You're never going to improve if you keep this up.

- Your feet look like they're glued to the ground! What's wrong with you?

- You keep making the same mistake. Stop slapping down on the ball!

- That was one of the worse performances I've ever seen. You didn't follow the game plan that I gave you. You did nothing to change.

This is far from an exhaustive list; I'm sure you can think of a lot more statements like these that can have a very negative impact. I've spoken with many adults who can still remember that one comment that a coach or a parent said to them when they were twelve that impacted their self-esteem.

We might also argue that this one-way style of instruction may impede a player's cognitive development over time, as it *reduces the player's active communication and engagement in the process.*

Best when you
teach new skills
and knowledge

However, the instructional style is appropriate for some players and has a time and place. This type of communication is best when you *need to teach and share new skills and knowledge*, when the player doesn't know what they need to do or how to do it. In addition, when you need to communicate a message quickly and specifically.

For example, coaches who are teaching a specific pattern for the first time to a group of beginners will need to be clear with their instructions about where to stand and how to move to execute this pattern effectively. In addition, when tour coaches are allowed to talk to their players on the 90-second change over, they may need to provide specific feedback and get to the point quickly to highlight blind spots, the communication most often used will be instructional.

One style doesn't
fit all

The problem is that *too many coaches use only this instructional communication style with all players and in all circumstances.* Furthermore, if they have achieved results in this way, they see little need to change.

The same applies to our workplaces. Managers who have grown up building their technical skills and become subject matter experts often have spent less time developing their communication skills. Because they're subject matter experts, everyone comes to them for their opinion, and they're more than happy to tell people what to do.

Over time, as they're promoted in their roles, directing and telling people what to do becomes an efficient style of management. It gets the task done, gets the job done, and gets results. *But I don't have to tell you that one size does not fit all.*

In fact, drawing on the experiences of many of my Podcast guests, myself, and Natalie, I can almost guarantee that our ability to adopt a more coachee-centred style of communication will get better results.

Once you add this style into your coaching toolkit, you can then use a combination of approaches based on the situation and the person in front of you.

| Coachee-centred communication | The *coachee-centred* communication style can often be used interchangeably with terms like collaborative, partnering, guided discovery, enquiry, and questioning. |

This communication style is two-way; rather than telling and directing, *the coach asks great questions like we have seen in this book to bring out the best in their players.* The player is more responsible for their decisions and actions beyond simply following instructions.

This alternative communication style *invites greater player input to the how, why, and what of learning,* with the coach acting as more of a facilitator of the learning. In terms of communication, you'll hear good quality questions, rather than the old yelling and telling. This helps encourage the player to become more *self-aware, to do their own problem-solving and explore solutions to various challenges.*

Like the instructional approach, the coachee-centred approach is not used with all players, all the time. But it is certainly preferred when we want to activate the player's learning and it creates a more fun, motivating, and empowering learning environment because the player is actively engaged.

As tennis influencer and coach, **Ema Burgic Bucko** shared on *The Coaching Podcast,* 'A great coach must have a connection with their player for the communication to be a two-way street. As a coach, you need to constantly ask questions and be curious.'

This is coming from a coach who grew up in a small village in Bosnia under the instructional style of teaching and while she had success as a player (7 time all-American), Ema understands the importance of balancing your communication.

> *Coachee-centred is much more common in workplaces*

Not surprisingly, the ***instructional communication*** style of coaching that I described first is what most people associate with coaching. I think this is because most people, when they think about coaching, think about sports coaching and this style is what they have experienced or witnessed.

However, ***the coachee-centred approach is more common in our workplaces.*** In fact, Natalie has spent the last 20 years teaching this approach to leaders and managers to enable them to move away from directing and telling their teams and move towards empowering, engaging, and promoting decision-making and innovation from their team members. Go into any workplace that has implemented a culture of coaching in the workplace and you'll see the coachee-centred style of communication.

This style was developed and popularised by legends like Sir John Whitmore in his book ***Coaching for Performance***. Whitmore was originally a successful motor-sports driver and tennis coach. He shared with Natalie that at the time, over 30 years ago, he wanted to get away from directing and telling in his coaching.

Whitmore noticed much better results on the tennis court and with the executive that he was working with when he adopted a style that included asking questions and allowing the coachee to find their answers.

To the tennis coaches and sports coaches reading this book, I guarantee this change in your approach will reap rewards with your players like you have never seen before. ***This is what the tennis world needs to learn from corporate workplaces.***

Stepping off the tennis court made me a better coach

As I've admitted, I wasn't always using a coachee-centred style of communication in my coaching, and it was something that I had to study. I got this opportunity during a year of study, which I undertook when I felt burnt out with the game and was considering a career change. In fact, this was one of the biggest sliding doors moments in my career.

My problem at the time was that I felt like I could only relate to half of my players. This was the catalyst for removing myself from an environment that was so familiar to me for so many years. Although I didn't realise this at the time, I simply didn't have enough strategies and resources in my coaching tool kit. *It took stepping off the tennis court to help me become a better coach. My experiences changed my outlook forever.*

The first course that I enrolled into was the Diploma of Workplace and Business Coaching [6] with a company called The Open Door Coaching Group (Open Door). I had such a thirst to better understand human development and behaviour that I went on to complete further study in a range of techniques including emotional intelligence, life coaching, neuro-linguistic programming (NLP), and mBraining.

This was when I first met my co-author and the Chief Executive Officer of Open Door, Natalie Ashdown. I will never forget the time when Natalie delivered one of the most impactful coaching sessions I had ever witnessed. Her style was completely coachee-centred.

Natalie asked questions like an artist paints a picture. *She asked great questions that allowed the coachee to find the answers that came from within them,* rather than telling, directing, advising, or mentoring the coachee. Under her guidance, I have learned how to ask better questions that bring out the best in my players and the people I work with in the corporate world.

Change your communication based on learning styles

The next critical communication concept that changed the way I coach was to fully immerse myself in ***understanding the four main learning styles and how to change my communication based on the learning styles.*** There is a lot of research on learning styles, and I admit some of it says that the generalisations are unfounded. But for me, they really make a difference and that's why I'm sharing this knowledge. The main four ways we learn are through ***visual, auditory, kinaesthetic*** and ***auditory-digital*** preferences. Now whilst we learn using ***all*** the different learning styles, some players will have a preference, as summarised:

Visual preference: Players with a visual preference learn best by visual clues - being shown or observing an activity and visualising their actions.

Auditory: Players with an auditory preference learn best through verbal clues that they are hearing and sounds around them, for example, the sound of the ball hitting the middle of the racquet.

Kinaesthetic: Some players learn best by just doing the activity and getting the feel of the activity. They want to get a grip on the equipment and get going with hitting, rather than talking about it.

Auditory-digital: Some players learn best when things first make sense to them. There is a clear purpose, structure, and process that is backed up by facts and figures.

One of the best activities to do is to think about one of your players and try to work out their preference. Do they respond best to you when you first:

- Demonstrate the activity to show the player what to do?
- Verbally explain the activity?
- Let them just jump in and have a go?
- Explain the purpose, process, and structure of the activity to ensure that it makes sense?

Learning style can be a little tricky to work out. Actually, ***players will learn through all the learning styles, even if they have a preference.*** But understanding the different learning styles is worth the effort to enable you to become a better communicator.

Adapting your style makes all the difference

I can recall many times where adapting my style made all the difference with my clients. One client in particular was Heather, whom I started coaching when she signed up to run her first marathon in New York City.

We started working together around high performance and specifically around mindset because her mindset had taken a battering from interactions with her previous personal trainer. She had completely lost her confidence.

In terms of her communication preference and personality, she was the opposite to mine. I adapted my tone to be more calming, slowed done my excitement when talking about her awesome goal, and went about bridging the gap between where she was at currently and where she wanted to go.

In addition, by asking her questions, I worked out that she learned best by seeing what had to be done (using videos and demonstrations) and by my giving her a step-by-step process to help things make sense. She also enjoyed 'homework' questions that would help her reflect and practice what we talk about. Very quickly, ***I could feel her relax into the collaborative coaching process.***

A lot of my coaching was also about helping her to turn some of the frequent and negative commands from her previous running coach into empowering beliefs. She needed technical information about running, ***but most importantly she needed a coach that would positively support her mindset in a way that worked for her.*** One session at a time, and by following her motto of one step at a time, she was able to achieve her dream goal and so much more.

Increase the impact of our communication

The same applies to the workplace. I often wonder why most communications in the workplace are sent in written form and mostly over email. It seems we have lost the knack of just picking up the phone. We all know that much of what is communicated is lost in the email translation and all too often *messages can be interpreted in the wrong way.*

We will *increase the impact of our communication if we adapt our style to suit all four learning preferences of our team members.* This means if we're sending particularly important communications, then we should be thinking about communicating in writing, talking to people, catching up with them face-to-face and making sure that anything we communicate has a step-by-step process that makes sense.

If we adapt our communications, they are more likely to be received in the manner that we had hoped for and are more likely to be understood. *And we know that better communication leads to less conflict, fewer errors, and higher performance in the workplace.*

Avoid a one-dimensional coaching style

In the early phases of my coaching career, I generally coached based on how I personally learnt best - through movement, which is the kinaesthetic mode. I predominantly had just this one style when delivering messages.

This, of course, worked well with players who were similar in learning preference and style to me. *But it created a one-dimensional style of coaching.* Unless the player was similar in personality and learning preference to me, then I wasn't having much success in bringing out the best in these players.

It wasn't until I took time away from the game altogether that the 'aha' moments began flowing in my direction. One particular day, I was surrounded by five extraordinary women and business coaches (Erina, Jen, Marisa, Helen, and Anna) from my Open Door coaching class. I remember thinking to myself:

Aha, the moral of the story is that I need to *change the way I communicate* to bring out the best in my players.

I don't mean a complete personality change but I do mean increasing my skills and coaching tools so that *I can adapt and create learning environments that unlock the potential that lives within the players* that I'm *fortunate enough to be able to impact.*

> *Change won't happen over night, but it is worth it.*

Changing my communication style from being instructional to more coachee-centred and learning about preferences did not happen overnight. This is a challenge for managers in the workplace who, as I have mentioned, have achieved a lot of success with the instructional, directing, and telling style. *But I can assure you that a focus on your communication is worth the effort.*

Someone who truly understands this message is Danish tennis coach and sports psychology consultant, **Adam Blicher**, who shared with me his worst coaching moment when he was coaching a group of players in Spain. When he realised that his one-dimensional style of communication was not working and that he was not skilled enough to bring out their best. This experience caused him to spark his curiosity and adapt his communication style. Adam said 'I now coach a lot more through analogies and metaphors that I feel will best serve my students.'

Moving to a coachee-centred style brings out the best in the person you're working with - enabling them to become more self-aware, make decisions and innovate.

Adapting your style ensures that messages are received in the way that you intended; it helps with influencing and reduces conflict. And as I've emphasised throughout the book, if we want to be great coaches then we must be working on our communication.

As **Peter McCraw** said: 'Effective coaching is not what you say, but what they hear. Not what you show them, but what they see. Not what you do, but what they do.'

In the end, the value is in how we communicate.

| *Your reflection* | **Now is the time to reflect on your communication skills:** |

What style of communication comes most naturally to you?

How would you describe your communication style?

What feedback have you received on your communication style?

What has to change about your communication style to make you a better coach?

How do you learn best?

Think of team members; what are their learning styles? How can you adapt your style to meet their needs?

Practice 10: Resilience

I think anyone can coach in any sport when things are going well; that's the easy part. But when things are difficult, how do you address those issues?'

Darren Cahill
Former ATP World No. 22 tennis player, tour coach,
and legendary television commentator

When it's time to use your secret weapon

It was the under 14s World Junior Tennis Competition and the Asia-Oceania leg was being played on our home courts at Melbourne Park, Australia. I was the team coach, and the team was seeded number one. We were confident of bringing home the championship glory.

I had slept off and on for no more than an hour at a time the night before the opening game because of the *pressure and expectation* of the occasion as the leader of the team. I had spent the night rehearsing strategies and coaching prompts in my head, whilst at the same time acknowledging that there is *no greater honour than to wear the Australian green and gold uniform.*

On game day, I could also sense the tension within the players as they wanted this win 'badly'. But the accumulated pressure was becoming too much for the players; at the end of day one, we had lost to the unseeded Chinese Taipei team. Our shot at the under 14s triumph seemed destined to be a sad memory.

Throughout the day, there had been a lot of tears amongst the team members, as each lost set put more emphasis on winning the next and amplified the pressure situation we found ourselves in. However, despite the pending doom, *we had a secret weapon, and it was time to use it.*

I believe I can fly

In the lead-up to the event, the team had been working on developing our resilience, and *it was time to exercise that skill.*

We found a private space behind the back of one of the courts, the furthest away from any of the main action, and pulled ourselves into a tight huddle. One of the team members pulled out her portable stereo player and we listened to our team song, *I Believe I Can Fly.* Some of the words from the song include, 'I believe I can fly. I believe I can touch the sky. If I can see it, then I can do it. *If I just believe it, there's nothing to it.'*

No one said a word as we connected with the words of the song and we started to sway and then dance around. Tennis is filled with opportunities for resilience to come to the foreground; there was *no greater opportunity than the present.* It was in this moment that we had to remind each other that one of the most important attributes that we would demonstrate was resilience. And at the same time, we needed to acknowledge that *somehow in the heat of battle during the day, we had forgotten to call on our resilience.*

We had lost on day one, but we still had a chance to qualify and head to Europe for the International Tennis Federation World Junior Tennis Competition finals. As we grooved to our song, I could feel the energy within the group begin to shift and we were able to let out our stresses. At the same time, we reframed the tears and the doubts to words of inspiration and reminded ourselves that *bouncing back was one of our superpowers.*

You can imagine there was a lot of girl power talk and a lot of 'I've got your back' and 'We got this.' Rather than beating each other up, we reinforced our team mantras, put our arms around each other, and almost yelled out the words together.

From the outside looking in, it might have seemed like a lot of 'rah rah'. But from the inside of that huddle, we were summoning our weapon - our resilience, *our driving force to get up and play well when the odds were against us.*

Reinforce your strengths in order to bounce back

The next morning, we arrived a full hour earlier than all the other teams and warmed up together. *We reinforced each other's strengths and our ability to bounce back.* And over the course of the next four days we went on to finish third in the Asia-Oceania draw, allowing us to qualify for the world championships in Prostejov, Czech Republic. Later that year we fought hard, brought our resilience with us, and finished sixth overall in the World Junior Tennis Competition finals.

One of the players on that team, **Johanna Konta**, went on to reach a career-high WTA singles ranking of No. 4 in the world. I had the opportunity many years later to talk to Johanna about those early championship days and how the players' and my own alignment around the value of resilience was a strong part of our success.

Johanna also commented that *the resilience skills she learned during those formative years have carried over well beyond our very memorable team experience.*

Another example from a tour coach who values resilience is coach **Louis Cayer**. Louis has had tremendous success with over 44 years as a tennis coach, especially in doubles, and he is a member of the Canadian Tennis Hall of Fame. On *The Coaching Podcast* he made an unforgettable comment, that is, 'We teach people, tennis. Not tennis to people.'

Louis backed up this comment with a story that he shared about a time that Andy and Jamie Murray did not do as well as they had expected at the Olympics. Louis said to Jamie, 'You know what? The best way to bounce back from that *is for you to go and win the US Open and finish number one.*' Even though Louis thought that this was a long shot for the pair to finish number one, Jamie replied, 'Okay, let's do it.' And that is exactly what happened.

Louis went on to say that the lesson in this story is that you can always find a reason to get motivated when things go well. However, overcoming a disappointing loss by focusing on your strengths and *being able to find a reason to get motivated* to bounce back are the cornerstones to building your resilience.

> *If you dwell on every lost point you're never going to be successful*

Tennis is a game that especially rewards *resilience, rather than perfection.* With 128 people in a Grand Slam draw, only one person can win the tournament. We learn early in our careers that tennis is one of those sports that will reveal, with every point, the character of coaches and players.

For example, in 2015, Roger Federer (who finished the year at World No. 3) and Serena Williams (who finished at World No. 1) were virtually unstoppable. Yet, they had won a total of only 55% of their points throughout the year [7]. To lose 45% of the points and still win means that *you need to win the critical points and keep bouncing back point after point.*

All players and coaches learn from early in their careers that *if you dwell on each lost point, you are never going to be successful.* Nick Bollettieri summarised this perfectly when he once said 'One trait that all champions share in common is that they are upset when they miss a shot that they know they can make. But they have this uncanny ability to *get over it quickly and focus all their energy on the next point.*'

In tennis if you make a mistake, you don't have a lot of time to stop and reflect. In the 20 to 25 seconds between points, the player needs to be thinking about how they will play the next point. If an easy shot is missed, we need the ability to get over ourselves quickly and call on our resilience. This is what I refer to as *micro-moments of resilience*. It is the ability to take no longer than three to five seconds to release the emotion from the previous point, think about your tactics for the next point, and then return to the present and compete.

This was demonstrated in the words of our loveable fictional coach, Ted Lasso, when he is coaching one of his superstar athletes he says, 'Do you know what the happiest animal on earth is? It's a goldfish. It has a ten-second memory. Be a goldfish, Sam.' I realise that this is easier said than done but investing in coaching tools to help your players in this area will definitely pay off.

Contrast this to other workplaces, outside of sport, where if you make an error, you can reflect on the error. You can call a meeting, review processes and procedures, conduct a collaborative problem-solving exercise, and discuss the best option or way forward. You can take your time to review just what went wrong and make apologies if needed.

In tennis, in the heat of the moment, this isn't possible. *Players must tap into their resilience in a heartbeat.* If not, before you know it, you can be 1-4 down and facing the end of the set or even the match.

> *Focus on the process and on giving your best effort*

These concepts were echoed during my interview on *The Coaching Podcast* and during a Tennis Australia workshop with **Darren Cahill**, Australian tennis legend and coach to some of the world's greatest tennis players.

Darren has coached Simona Halep to win two Grand Slam titles and to reach World No. 1. Before Simona, Cahill helped Lleyton Hewitt and Andre Agassi to reach World No. 1. Darren says that the top 10 players in the world have several traits in common including resilience, which he defines as the ability to overcome adversity.

As an example, Darren went on to describe that in 2017, Simona was one set and 3-0 up against Jelena Ostapenko in the final of the French Open. Darren made the mistake of thinking 'We got this' only to see Simona collapse in the set and lose the match. It wasn't until long after the debrief of the event, thanks to the support of the team, that Darren reflected on the way that he was communicating with her.

In particular, Darren's direct approach was putting pressure on Simona, and this pressure was being exaggerated by her Romanian culture. He explained how a typical Romanian mindset is to look at negative things and multiple this by ten times. Consequently, *any feedback that Darren was providing, would be multiplied several times over in the negative* in the mind of his player. Add to this the national pressure of being the best Romanian tennis player across both the male and female draws. *Darren knew he had to change his approach.*

Darren needed to dig deep and call on his own resilience to problem solve and to help his player bounce back from the loss. He thought he had to do this by showing strong leadership, directing the team, and making key decisions for Simona. However, he describes this approach as one of his worst coaching moments and he realised he was being a little too 'old school' and therefore out of balance.

So instead, Darren switched his coaching style with Simona to *focus on the process and giving your best effort rather than the results.* She worked on her resilience to be strong, stay smart, and keep fighting. They worked together to enable Simona to be herself, not another version of another player, and on the culture of the team surrounding her.

Darren believes that getting the culture right must come before leadership; he was now coaching his player through her eyes, rather than through his own eyes, as we have discussed in our previous chapter. Through this, they *built the resilience to fight to win the grand slams.*

Sharing victory and defeat

Many coaches talk about sliding doors moments, when they've been fired by a player and must change and turn direction immediately. **Patrick Mouratoglou**, former coach of Serena Williams, talked to me about how as coaches we're measured by our results and how winning matters.

He said, 'We are accountable for our players' achievements. It is *up to us to take responsibility for them, both in victory and in defeat.'*

Patrick shared an example of this from the time that he asked Arsène Wenger how he managed to stay manager of Arsenal Football Club for 20 years. Wenger said it was because the team had never lost three matches in a row. The same applies to the cutthroat world of tennis.

'If your player is losing', explains Patrick, 'you're out. *Most coaches last about a year with a top player.'* It's for this reason, that as coaches, the resilience needs to start from within ourselves.

On **The Coaching Podcast** Patrick also shared a time when he really had to call on his resilience. Patrick worked for Bob Brett's Tennis Academy in France for many years, until one day Bob announced he was leaving the academy. Patrick said he felt so disappointed to lose his mentor and stop working with his long-term friend that he really wanted to quit. In fact, he wanted to stop the academy altogether because he felt like there was no point to continue. However, at that time, many of the players, including Marcos Baghdatis, asked him to stay. This gave him so much enthusiasm and will to go on that now the Mouratoglou Tennis Academy is one of the most famous in the world.

> *Never feel down for more than an hour*

From my own experience, resilience is something that has grown in me overtime. I used to say to myself, 'Never feel down for more than half a day' and over time I changed this to *'Never be down for more than an hour.'* But as I have mentioned, in elite sport, the window must be reduced to seconds. The more we work with our players on this, the better they're able to adapt.

One such player comes to mind from back in my days of coaching. His name was Michael, and he was a talented and highly competitive young player. His major problem was an inability to control his emotions. In the early days he would constantly be in tears, crying whenever something wasn't going his way. As his coach, it was hard to watch. It was *harder still to listen to the 'here we go again' comments from onlookers and to know that I was responsible for building his resilience.*

Michael would come off the court, complaining about how every element of the match and the environment was unfair. It was unfair that he had to play on the far court; that his opponent had his dad watching and coaching; that his shoelaces would come loose during the game and distract him; that the roving umpire would overrule his line calls 'all the time' and it was clear he was favouring his opponent; and that waiting for the courts to be swept meant that he was cooling down too quickly.

It was during one of his post-match rants about how everything about tennis was unfair, that I had a new idea. The next week, *I introduced Michael to the Unfair Cards.*

'You think life is unfair? That tennis is unfair?' I asked him in the 'things are about to get real' tone and didn't wait for the answer. 'Well guess what? We're going to build your ability to suck it up and deal with it. And forget the tears. Your days of crying because things are unfair are over.' I watched him carefully, *holding my breath and not knowing how he would respond to my directness.*

But we were at a critical turning point because I knew that my reputation as a coach at the local club and his reputation as a player were both on the line. I noticed his bottom lip start to tremble a little and he took a long breath inwards as we stared at each other intently.

'Right then,' I said, after what seemed like ages, but was only a few tense seconds. 'Let me introduce you to the Unfair Cards.'

We took the next 15 minutes together to write down all the 'unfair' things that Michael had experienced over his short career, with each item dedicated to its own card. Once that was done, we started to play some points and without warning, I could pull out an Unfair Card. For example, I pulled out the 'player calls the ball out, when clearly it was in' card. Then when Michael hit a winner that was clearly within the lines, I would call the ball out.

The first time I did this he flew into a rage, grabbing the tennis ball and smacking it so hard it went over the dividing mesh across the neighbouring courts, nearly smashing the clubhouse window. The second time, he let out some expletives and I simply said 'Hey, life is unfair. What are you going to do about it? And by the way, you can go and retrieve that ball now.'

Interestingly, as he turned to trudge off to collect the balls, his shoulders were stooped and he was dragging his feet, but there were no tears. *Even with this simple start, his behaviour had changed.*

My other favourite examples were simply catching the ball mid-flight and declaring, 'I win the point.' Or making him stop and actually take off one shoe (representing something going wrong with his shoes that used to throw him off this game) and play out the point.

Within a really short period of time, I would say less than five or six lessons, Michael, to his credit, had built his resilience. He was more ready and prepared for anything that was thrown at him during the match. He would hear my words 'What are you going to do about it?' ringing in his ears and he had the game style to **call on his problem-solving skills to answer the questions.**

Michael went on to be one of the toughest local competitors and learned how to push himself beyond his self-imposed boundaries. He had wonderful and supportive parents who trusted the coaching process. It was an honour to play a role in his early formative years.

Michael is now in the financial services industry, and I often wonder whether his lessons on the court set him up to deal with many other setbacks that he might face throughout his career. I'd certainly like to think that they did.

> *Acknowledging there will be setbacks; not everything will go your way*

As I mentioned, it seems that in the workplace, we have more time to bounce back from setbacks than we do in tennis. However, that doesn't make building resilience any less important.

For an organisation, team, or individual to achieve long-term results, they need to **acknowledge that there will be setbacks; not everything will go our way or be perfect.** That's where the resilience kicks in - to enable a focus on high performance and achieving organisational goals, despite the setbacks.

As **Darren Cahill** offered: 'I think anyone can coach in any sport or business when things are going well, that's the easy part. But when things are difficult and you have some culture issues, some difficult losses, or you have an individual player within a team that keeps making the same mistake over and over again, how do you address those issues? That's where your leadership and coaching makes a difference.'

It comes as no surprise that Darren Cahill, Ric Charlesworth and performance specialist tennis coach, **Simon Wheatley** all rank resilience in their top three responses as to what makes a great coach.

We can take two important lessons from tennis. Firstly, ***the team member needs to keep the situation in perspective.*** In tennis we acknowledge, yes, they might have been slow to that one ball; but it is just that - one ball. The same applies in the workplace. Yes, the team member has made a mistake; but (hopefully) it is just a mistake, and we can learn from it and move on. The next approach will be different.

Secondly, it is critical to ***watch the language that we use.*** Players will hold onto one-liners that the coach says, but taken out of context, use that one-liner to confirm their negative thoughts. This erodes their confidence and their resilience.

For example, if the coach says, 'You're too slow getting to that ball,' I've seen children who start to repeat that line as an excuse for every ball they miss.

One of my players would smack the racquet on the side of their shoe in frustration and say, 'I'm too slow.'

When I questioned what or why they continuously said that they replied, *'That's what my last coach said.'*

In tennis, as is the case in the workplace, we need to frame our statements in the positive, stating what we want to see. For example, in tennis we might say, 'How can you explode towards the net when you're chasing down a drop shot?' Notice the word explode triggers an emotion and a positive word for the player to connect with.

In the workplace we might say 'How can we make sure we deliver excellent customer service next time?'

In addition, connecting to and reminding team members of our purpose, our goals and the process helps to draw on our resilience. It is a balancing act, but an important one to get right. Through empathy and kindness, we create a safe environment of trust. We will find opportunities to build resilience, to not dwell on failures and to work out ways to overcome setbacks.

Coaches I interviewed also provided us with great questions:

Tennis coach **Darren Cahill**: 'How much do you focus on the weaknesses compared to the strengths of a player?'

Former ATP No. 100 tennis player and motivational coach **Jeff Salzenstein**: 'How do you handle stress?'

Teen education speaker and coach **Sonya Karras**: 'How do you handle the "Nos"?'

Track and field coach **Vicky Huyton**: 'How many times did you get knocked down and where did you find the strength to get back up?'

NFL Coach **Jay Gruden**: 'How do people handle adversity? Because everyone can handle success easily. It's adversity. It's when teams don't do as well as expected, when players don't do as well as expected. How do you get motivated to work even harder on a daily basis?'

Time to start walking your talk	Finally, as I have talked about throughout the book, ***these practices need to start with ourselves.*** I found myself recently reminiscing on moments of resilience, but unfortunately,

those memories were coming to me whilst I was in the middle of our golf club championships. As a result, I had lost concentration and hit a long and lofty ball straight into the water. From there, on the next three holes, I scored two double bogeys and then a triple bogey.

Prior to these holes I had been in clear second place and now I was listening to myself, almost like an out-of-body experience, to my internal dialogue telling me I had stuffed up, I was going to lose second place, and it would be all over for another year. ***The irony hit me like a slap in the face, as I stuffed my driver back into its sock and rammed it into my bag.***

I had just been working on this very chapter with Natalie and recounting stories of the need for resilience in ourselves and in our players. Walking down the fairway, I laughed out loud. I took hold of my spare hair tie that I always kept around my wrist, pulling it out to the point that it almost broke and let it go with a sharp 'thwack' back against my wrist to change my state.

'Resilience,' I said to myself. 'Time to start walking your talk, Coach Emma.'

I took some deep breaths, spread my shoulders, lifted my head, and started to stride confidently to the next hole. At the same time, I was visualising my next shot - importantly, the finish of the shot - the way that my body would be positioned if I hit a brilliant shot.

I scored a birdie on that next hole and with my resilience in play and my confidence restored, went on to come second in the club championships. Importantly, I achieved so much more that day than any of the associated accolades. I was reminded of the constant need for us as players and coaches to always be ready to tap into our resilience, to call on those driving forces that help us dig ourselves out of holes. ***As coaches we can't just talk about resilience; we must walk our talk.***

Your reflection	Now is the opportunity to reflect on your resilience by thinking about the following questions:

Describe a time when you have called upon your resilience?

How did you access this resilience?

What difference has this moment made to your life?

What were the key lessons from the moment?

What are your driving forces?

What do you call upon when the going gets tough?

What do you say to yourself?

Where does your resilience and fighting force come from?

Game, Set, Match

'Are you willing to dedicate your life to your profession?'

Nick Bollettieri
Legendary tennis coach

> The learning
> doesn't stop

Any one tennis player will play hundreds of matches from the time they first pick up the racquet to the time they retire. The same goes for coaches. I have no idea how many tennis matches I've watched, but at the end of each match, the umpire will announce 'game, set, match' to the winner.

With that, the chapter that is represented by that match is finished. *But the learning doesn't stop.* The game is analysed, debriefed, reviewed, re-watched, picked apart, and discussed long after the bags were packed on the tennis court and the racquets sent for re-stringing.

The same goes for this book and high performance in our workplaces.

You may have come to the end of the book, but there is work for us all to do, to become the best coaches we can become.

Judy Murray posed some great questions for us to continue to think about:

- What's next for me?

- Who can I learn from?

- Who can I influence?

- Who can I share with?

This is what I encourage you to do with the practices in this book.

Coaching is a privilege. Sharing in the successes and the difficult times with your teams whether it's on the court or in your corporate workplaces is an even bigger privilege.

Our 10 top practices are not something that we just read about and, as I mentioned in the very beginning, say, 'Oh yeah, I do that'; ***they are practices that we must continue to reflect upon and refine.*** In addition, as we mentioned in the opening chapter, 'talent is not nearly as important as execution'. Therefore, reflecting and taking action in the direction of your goals and dreams will help you unleash your potential.

Speaking of dreams, it seems only fitting that 24 years after I first met Gabe Jaramillo he asked for us all to reflect on the question, 'What's your dream?'

We wish for you to keep believing in the power of dreams - BIG dreams and then go and make them happen!

The ball is in your court to take action.

Go curious and enjoy your coaching.

| Final Reflection | With that in mind, it is time for you to capture key action items that you will undertake to build on the 10 top practices. |

We hope you enjoy celebrating your personal achievements as you build high performance workplaces with a renewed focus on the 10 top practices.

It is time now for your final set of reflection questions:

As a result of investing your time in reading this book, what will do for yourself in the next 24 hours?

What will you do for one of your players/team members in the next seven days?

Who do you think needs to read this book next?

Who can you share the top 10 practices with?

What key messages are you going to share with a fellow coach?

From the top 10 practices, what are your strengths as a coach (minimum of three)?

From the top 10 practices, what are your areas for development?

In the next 90 days, what will you commit to working on?

In one to a maximum of three words, what do you think makes a great coach?

Finally take some time to dream big. What's your dream?

Coach Reference

The coaches who are named in this book are listed below in alphabetical order (first name basis). They were either interviewed by myself, guests on *The Coaching Podcast* or I met them at coaching conferences and asked the guiding question.

Their responses to this question, 'In one to a maximum of three words, what makes a great coach?' are listed below.

I am always fascinated by how people interpret the question, that is, some coaches give three different qualities and others attempt to summarize their thinking in a three-word statement, such as, 'Someone who listens.'

I'm extremely grateful to the 500 plus wonderful coaches who have shared their wisdom and I will continue to collect the answers to this question.

Adam Blicher - Expectation, Adapt, Environment
Aiden M. A. Thornton - 'Wise decision-making.'
Aish Ravi - Passion, Care, Kind
Ajay Pant - Trust, Trust, Trust
Aleksandra Krunić - Knowledge, Passion, Understanding
Alicia Molik - 'One that listens.'
Allistair McCaw - Understanding, Energy, Trust
Andy Scantland - 'Deep level listening.'
Anne Pankhurst - 'Understand the player.'
Anni Miller - 'Real authentic.'
Barb Van Hare - Love, Listening, Curiosity
Becky Magnotta - Curiosity, Joy, Community
Belinda Colaneri - Empathy, Confident, Teacher
Bethanie Mattek-sands - 'Reading energy.'
Bill Riddle - Passion, Passion, Passion
Carl Maes - Content, Empathy, Integrity
Carla McKenzie - Passion, Listens, Relatable

Carol Fox - Intention, Heart-space, (be) True
Casey Dellacqua - Communicator, Respect, Fun
Charles Hardman - 'Ability to learn.'
Chie Tougas - Love, Learn, Grow
Chris Anstey - 'Ability to listen.'
Chris Michalowski - Passion, Compassion, Empathy
Chuck Gill - Empathy, goal-driven
Claire Nelson - Vision, Passion, Empowerment
Claude Silver - Patience, Empathy, Action
Cliff Mallett - Care, Challenging, Curious
Craig Cignarelli - Inspiring, Curious
Damian Carmody-Stephens - 'Nothing and everything.'
Daniel Flynn - 'Calls blind spots.'
Darren Cahill - Listen, Resilience, Evolve
David Goffin - Creativity, Experience, Knowledge
David McNamara - Enthusiasm, Energy, Education
David Wheadon - Empathy, Teaching, People Management
Dean Hollingworth - Care, Knowledge, Passion
Debbie Kirkwood - Passion, Excellence, Integrity
Diana Cutaia - Empathy, Humility, Self-reflection
Dinara Safina - Discipline, Humility, Passion
Donato Campagnoli - 'Power to empower
Ema Burgic Bucko - Energy, Connection, Communication
Emilio Sánchez - Listen, Values, Trust
Erin Allard - Empathy, Detailed, Space
Gabe Jaramillo - Passion, Perseverance, Knowledge/Wisdom
Gigi Fernandez - Listen, Communicate, Motivate
Hana Mandlíková - Love
Helen Rice - Empathy, Hunger, Passion
Helen Thompson - Compassion, Empathy, Believe
Helena Suková - Empathy, Knowledge, Patience
Howard Moore - 'Words with impact.'
Jack Groppel - Character, Curiosity, Connection
Jared Bull - Curiosity, Challenging, Compassion
Jay Gruden - Listen, Motivate, Adjust
Jeff Salzenstein - Passion, Awareness, Growth Mindset
Jen Brice - Listening, Curiosity, Empathy

Jim Harp - Sincere, Educated, Purposeful
Jim Loehr - 'Transcendent purpose.'
Jim Rembach - 'Person before power.'
Joe Dinoffer - Communicate
Johanna Konta - Open, Values
John Birrell - 'Non-stop learners.'
John Bordon - Listening, Preparation, Sincerity
John Buchanan - Passion, Integrity, Challenge
Jon Yeo - Listening, Faith, Patience
Jorge Capestany - Flexibility, Learner, Customisation
Juan-Pablo Abarca - Passion, Simplicity
Judy Murray - Listens
Judy Sabah - Presence, Listening, Questions
Jules Hay - Communication, Relationships
Julie Gordon - Inspire, Motivate, Support
Justine Henin - Communication, Honest, Invested
Karen Deierhoi - Ownership, Empowerment, Belief
Ken Martel - 'For the athlete.'
Kenneth Bastiaens - Empathy, Open, Love
Kim Clijsters - Reliable, funny, respectful
Kim Miles - 'Accessing your intuition.'
Kris Soutar - Learner, Empathy, Love
Kyle LaCriox - Commitment, Passion, Loyalty
Laura Youngson - Caring, Energy, Motivational
Lauren Warden - 'Recognising individual motivation.'
Lisa Stone - Communication, Compassion, Commitment
Lorenzo Beltrame - Care, knowledge, confidence
Louis Cayer - Caring, Vision
Marley Woods - Curious, Listens, Positive
Manu 'Swish' Goswami - Empathy, Compassion, Gratitude
Margit Bannon - Creative, Grounded, Learner
Mark Draper - Consistency, Authenticity, Patience
Mark Jeffery - Love, Passion, Accountability
Mark McGregor - 'Affirming people's potential.'
Mary Pat Faley - Energy, Information, Caring
Mats Wilander - 'In the present.'
Meike Babel - 'Great listener.'

Melissa Mizer - 'Pure love.'
Michele Krause - Positive, Enthusiastic, Energy
Michelle Cleere - Positive, Encouraging, Authentic
Mitch Hewitt - 'Know your player.'
Nick Bollettieri - 'Knowing your student.'
Nicole Pratt - Care, Passion, Belief
Olga Harvey - 'Instils confidence.'
Oliver Luck - Love, Knowledge, Energy
Ollie Stephens - Patience, Understanding, Caring
Pat Van der Meer - Calming, Positive, Energy
Note: Pat responded on behalf of Denis Van der Meer
- Enthusiasm, Caring, Organisational
Patrick Mouratoglou - Hear, Results, Expectations
Piotr Unierzyski - Passion, Open Mind
PJ Simmons - Connection, Invested, Deliberate
Rebecca DiCello - Intuitive
Ric Charlesworth - Passion, Quality, Resilience
Robin Söderling - Listener, Determined, Love
Roger Crawford - 'Reaching higher.'
Roger Federer - 'Someone who listens.'
Sacha Kaluri - Support, Belief, Guidance
Sarah Stone - Caring, Emotional Intelligence, Empathy
Scott Rawlins - Passion, Obsessiveness, Love
Simon Blair - Energy, Empathy, Imagination
Simon Wheatley - Resilient, Leadership, Role-model
Sonya Karras - Authentic, Open
Steve Annacone - Believer, Listener, Teacher
Steve Barlow - Learning, Growth, Change
SyRae Weikle - Genuine, Confident, Caring
Tina Keown - Empathise, Listen, Encourage
Tina Samara - Passion, Patience, Knowledge
Tony Palafox - 'Know your player.'
Travis Bell - Empathy, Vision, Accountability
Urszula Radwanska - Patience, Motivation, Listening
Valorie Kondos Field - 'Know thy self.'
Vicky Huyton - Passion
Yasemin Ozsoy - Agile, Direction

Bibliography

[1] Tobias, R. (2009). Changing behaviour by memory aids: A social pyschological model of prospective memory and habit development tested with dynamic field data. *Psychological Review, 116(2)*, 408-438.

[2] Coprorate Leadership Council (2002). Building the High-performance Workforce - A Quantitative Analysis of the Effectiveness of Performance Management Strategies. *www.corporateleadershipcouncil.com*

[3] The video can be found here: https://vimeo.com/41343451

[4] Lara-Bercial & Mallet. (2016). Practices & Development Pathways of Serial Winning Coaches. *International Sports Coaching Journal*, 3, 221-239.

[5] Tennis Australia Coach Manual

[6] Latest version is the Diploma of Organisational Coaching (10835NAT), www.opendoorcoaching.com.au

[7] O'Shannessy. (2015). Brain Game Tennis. https://www.braingametennis.com/

Connect with us

EMMA DOYLE

What makes a great coach?
Energy, Empathy, Enjoyment

Website: www.emmadoyle.com.au
Email: info@emmadoyle.com.au

The Coaching Podcast - Coach for Success in Sport and Business
www.opendoorcoachingusa.com/podcasts/the-coaching-podcast

TEDx Talk
www.youtube.com/watch?v=Hu3tMg_Izzw

LinkedIn: linkedin.com/in/emma-doyle-41150215

Twitter: EmmaDoyleIII

NATALIE ASHDOWN

What makes a great coach?
Empathy, Listening, Curiosity

Website: www.opendoorcoaching.com.au
Email: info@opendoorcoaching.com.au

The Coaching Café Podcast
https://opendoorcoaching.com.au/blog/

Natalie's book: *Bring Out Their Best - Inspiring a Coaching Culture in Your Workplace* is available at www.opendoorcoaching.com.au

LinkedIn: linkedin.com/in/natalieashdown

Twitter: OpenDoorCoach